Development Team

Authors

Cheri Smith
Yale Secondary
School District 34 Abbotsford

Gary Davidson
School District 22 Vernon

Megan Ryan
Walnut Grove Secondary
School District 35 Langley

Chris Toth
St. Thomas More Collegiate
Burnaby, British Columbia

Program Consultant

Lionel Sandner
Edvantage Interactive

COPIES OF THIS BOOK MAY BE OBTAINED BY CONTACTING:

Edvantage Interactive

E-MAIL:
info@edvantageinteractive.com

TOLL-FREE FAX:
866.275.0564

TOLL-FREE CALL:
866.422.7310

EDVANTAGE
INTERACTIVE

AP Chemistry 2 WorkbookPLUS

ISBN 978-1-77249-676-5

Vice-President of Marketing: *Don Franklin*
Director of Publishing: *Yvonne Van Ruskenveld*
Design and Production: *Donna Lindenberg, Paula Gaube*
Editorial Assistance: *Rhys Sandner*
Proofreading: *Eva van Emden*

QR Code — What Is This?

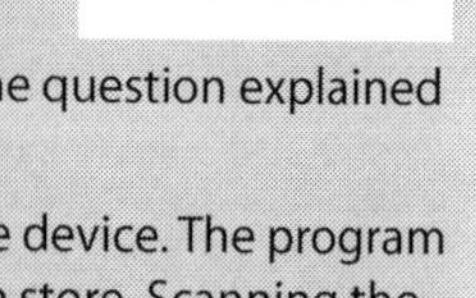

The image to the right is called a QR code. It's similar to bar codes on various products and contains information that can be useful to you. Each QR code in this book provides you with online support to help you learn the course material. For example, find a question with a QR code beside it. If you scan that code, you'll see the answer to the question explained in a video created by an author of this book.

You can scan a QR code using an Internet-enabled mobile device. The program to scan QR codes is free and available at your phone's app store. Scanning the QR code above will give you a short overview of how to use the codes in the book to help you study.

Note: We recommend that you scan QR codes only when your phone is connected to a WiFi network. Depending on your mobile data plan, charges may apply if you access the information over the cellular network. If you are not sure how to do this, please contact your phone provider or us at info@edvantageinteractive.com

AP Chemistry 2 WorkbookPLUS

EDVANTAGE INTERACTIVE

Contents

Welcome to AP Chemistry 2 Workbook*PLUS*

AP Chemistry 2 Workbook*PLUS* is a print and digital resource for classroom and independent study, aligned with the AP curriculum. You, the student, have three core components — this write-in workbook with the Traffic Lights learning strategy, QR codes to access AP Chemistry content and an interactive Online Study Guide.

AP Chemistry 2 Workbook*PLUS*

Chapter 3
Traffic Light Study Guide

Section	Page	I can ...	Red	Yellow	Gr
3.1	182	State the *first law of thermodynamics*.	○	○	
	183	State the *second law of thermodynamics*.	○	○	
	183 - 184	Write the *Boltzmann equation* and state the *third law of thermodynamics*.	○	○	
	184	State how a system's temperature affects its *thermal disorder* and its Δ thermal disorder when heat is added or removed.	○	○	
	185 - 186	Calculate the entropy change and thus determine the spontaneity of a reaction, given the reactants' and products' *standard entropies (S°)*.	○	○	
3.2	191 - 192	Provide the formula for the change of *Gibb's Free Energy (ΔG)* and relate a reaction's free energy to its spontaneity.	○	○	
	192, 196	Predict the spontaneity of a reaction, given the signs of ΔH and ΔS. in cases where those signs are the same, relate spontaneity to temperature.	○	○	
	193	Relate a reaction's change of Free Energy (ΔG) to the amount of recoverable energy it releases.	○	○	
	193	State the value of ΔG for a reaction at equilibrium.	○	○	
	194 - 195	Use the *Gibbs-Helmholtz Equation* to calculate a *Standard Free Energy Change (ΔG°)* at Standard Temperature.	○	○	
	196	Use *Free Energies of Formation* to calculate a Standard Free Energy Change (ΔG°) at Standard Temperature.	○	○	
	197 - 198	Use the *Gibbs-Helmholtz Equation* to calculate a Standard Free Energy Change (ΔG) at Non-Standard Temperatures.	○	○	
3.3	205 - 206	Calculate the change of Free *Energy* (ΔG) for a reaction mixture with gaseous species at Non-Standard Pressures. Determine the direction the reaction will proceed to achieve equilibrium.	○	○	
	207 - 209	Convert a Standard Free Energy change (ΔG°) into K_{eq} (and vice-versa).	○	○	
	210	Draw diagrams showing how Free Energy changes during the course of exergonic and endergonic reactions at constant temperature.	○	○	

Why is Workbook*PLUS* different?

The Workbook*PLUS* is a combination of print and digital tools specifically designed to help you learn AP Chemistry.

At the start of each chapter is a learning strategy called Traffic Lights. Read the 'I can' statements and fill in the circle that best represents your understanding. Red means I don't get it; Yellow, I sort of get it; Green means I completely get it.

Use the QR codes on the Traffic Light pages to access digital content.

Use the Workbook*PLUS* to answer AP level questions.

Take online quizzes at edvantagescience.com to check your understanding.

Before any test you should have all green lights for the 'I can' statements. All green lights mean you're ready to go. Any red or yellow lights mean you need to study more, talk to your teacher, or take the review quizzes at edvantagescience.com.

Why use the Traffic Lights strategy to learn?

Learning is an extremely active and personal process. The Workbook*PLUS* keeps you focused on the correct material to learn.

Research has shown that physically interacting with your text to solve problems results in better comprehension and retention.

How to make this book work for you:

1. Review the Traffic Light Study guide to determine what you already know.
2. Do the Warm Ups to activate prior knowledge.
3. Scan the QR code for AP Chemistry content and read the relevant sections
4. Do the Review Questions by writing down the full answers. This is important! Scan the **QR codes** or go to the **Online Study Guide** to see video worked solutions by *AP Chemistry 2* Workbook*PLUS* authors.
5. Try the **Online Study Guide** for online quizzes, PowerPoints, and more.

For more information on how to purchase your own personal copy
info@edvantageinteractive.com

AP Chemistry 2 Online Study Guide (OSG)

What is an Online Study Guide?

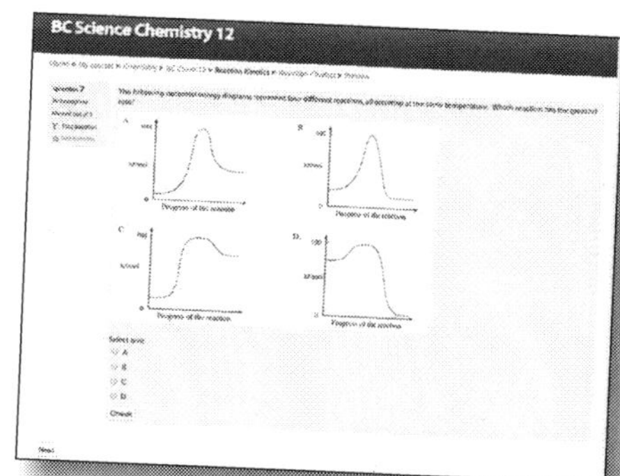

It's an interactive, personalized, digital, mobile study guide to support the Workbook*PLUS*.

The **Online Study Guide** or OSG, provides access to online quizzes, PowerPoint notes, and video worked solutions.

Need extra questions, sample tests, a summary of your notes, worked solutions to some of the review questions? It's all here!

Access it where you want, when you want.

Make it your own personal mobile study guide.

What's in the Online Study Guide?

Scan this code for a quick tour of the OSG

- Online quizzes, multiple choice questions, exam-like tests with instant feedback
- PowerPoint notes: Key idea summary and student study notes from the textbook
- Video worked solutions: Select video worked solutions from the WorkText

If you have a smart phone or tablet, scan the QR code to the right to find out more.

Where is the Online Study Guide located?

www.edvantagescience.com

Should I use the Online Study Guide?

YES... if you want to do your best in this course.
The OSG is directly LINKED to the activities and content in the Workbook*PLUS*.
The OSG helps you learn what is taught in class.

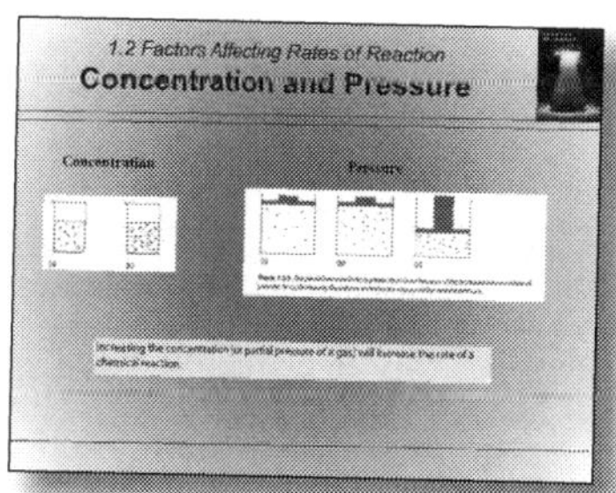

If your school does not have access to the Online Study Guide and you'd like more information — info@edvantageinteractive.com

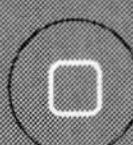

1 Reaction Kinetics

This chapter focuses on the following AP Big Idea from the College Board:

- Big Idea 4: Rates of chemical reactions are determined by details of the molecular collisions.

By the end of this chapter, you should be able to do the following:

- Demonstrate awareness that reactions occur at differing rates
- Experimentally determine rate of a reaction
- Demonstrate knowledge of collision theory
- Describe the energies associated with reactants becoming products
- Apply collision theory to explain how reaction rates can be changed
- Analyze the reaction mechanism for a reacting system
- Represent graphically the energy changes associated with catalyzed and uncatalyzed reactions
- Describe the uses of specific catalysts in a variety of situations

---

By the end of this chapter, you should know the meaning of these **key terms**:

- activated complex
- activation energy
- bimolecular
- catalyst
- catalytic converter
- collision theory
- ΔH notation
- elementary processes
- endothermic
- enthalpy
- enzymes
- exothermic
- heterogeneous catalysts
- homogeneous catalysts
- initial rate
- integrated rate law
- KE distribution curve
- kinetic energy (KE),
- metalloenzymes
- molecularity
- overall order
- potential energy (PE)
- product
- rate-determining step
- reactant
- reaction intermediate
- reaction mechanism
- reaction rate
- successful collision
- termolecular
- thermochemical equation

External tanks of liquid oxygen and hydrogen fuel react to create the energy needed to launch a rocket carrying the space shuttle.

Edvantage Science AP Chemistry 2

Chapter 1

Traffic Light Study Guide

Section	Page	I can ...	Red	Yellow	Green
1.1	2	Define *chemical kinetics*.	○	○	○
	3	Define *reaction rate*.	○	○	○
	4 - 5	Given a chemical reaction, describe a method(s) for measuring or monitoring its rate.	○	○	○
	3 - 4 6 - 7	Calculate reaction rates from both numerical and graphical data.	○	○	○
	6 - 7	Convert the rate of consumption or production of one species into that of another.	○	○	○
	8 -9	Use reaction rates to calculate the amount of reactant consumed or product formed in a given period of time.	○	○	○
1.2	16	Cite five factors that affect reaction rates.	○	○	○
	16	Describe and explain how reactant surface area affects the rates of *heterogeneous* reactions.	○	○	○
	16 - 17	Describe and explain how reactant concentrations affect reaction rates.	○	○	○
	17 - 18	Describe and explain how temperature affects reaction rates.	○	○	○
	18	Cite two properties of atoms and two properties of molecules that can affect their reactivity.	○	○	○
	19	Define a *catalyst*.	○	○	○
1.3	24 – 25	Write the general formula for a *rate law*. Identify the *rate constant* and the *reactant orders* in the formula.	○	○	○
	26	State *Collision theory*.	○	○	○
	27	Define *activation energy* (E_a).	○	○	○
	28	Draw 2 Collision Energy Diagrams representing the distribution of collision energies at two temperatures. Label the E_a for a supposed reaction. State what the areas under the curves represent and explain the relevance of this to reaction rates.	○	○	○
	28	Describe what the term *collision geometry* refers to and its relevance to reaction rates.	○	○	○
	28 - 30	State the external factors that affect reaction rates and explain in terms of collision theory how each impacts the reaction rate.	○	○	○
1.4	36 – 39	Describe how the initial rate of a reaction is determined from graphical data.	○	○	○
	37 – 38	Determine a *reaction's order* with respect to each reactant, its overall order, and its *rate law expression*, from tabular data.	○	○	○
	38 - 41	Determine a reaction's rate constant (k) from tabular data.	○	○	○

Edvantage Science AP Chemistry 2

Chapter 1

Traffic Light Study Guide

Section	Page	I can …	Red	Yellow	Green
1.5	45 - 47	For *first-order reactions*, use the *integrated rate law* to calculate the concentration of a reactant after a given time period or vice-versa.	○	○	○
	48 - 49	For *second-order reactions*, use the *integrated rate law* to calculate the concentration of a reactant after a given time period or vice-versa.	○	○	○
	50	Describe and explain the kinetics of a *zero-order reaction*.	○	○	○
	50 - 52	Determine a reaction's order (zero, first, or second) and its rate constant through graphical analysis.	○	○	○
	54- 54	Calculate the *half-life* ($t_{1/2}$) of a first-order reaction, given the rate constant (k) of the reaction.	○	○	○
	56 - 57	Describe how each half-life of a zero and a second-order reaction contrasts with the previous half-life.	○	○	○
	56 - 57	Calculate the half-lives of a zero and a second-order reaction, given the rate constants (k) of the reactions and the reactant concentrations.	○	○	○
1.6	65	Define *enthalpy*.	○	○	○
	66	Describe *endothermic* and *exothermic* reactions in terms of the relative energies involved in breaking the reactant bonds and forming the product bonds.	○	○	○
	66	Convert a thermochemical equation into one using a ΔH notation and vice-versa.	○	○	○
	67	Define *activated complex*.	○	○	○
	67	Describe the events and corresponding kinetic and potential energy conversions that occur as reactant molecules collide.	○	○	○
	67 – 68	Draw a *potential energy diagram* for an endothermic reaction and also one for an exothermic reaction. In each case, label the P.E. of the reactant(s), product(s), and activated complex, the activation energy (E_a), and the change of enthalpy (ΔH).	○	○	○
	68 – 70	Read and label a potential energy diagram in the reverse direction, i.e. for the reverse reaction.	○	○	○
	71	Describe how a catalyst generally increases a reaction's rate. Illustrate this on a potential energy diagram.	○	○	○

For more support in AP Chemistry 2, go to edvantagescience.com

Edvantage Science AP Chemistry 2

Chapter 1

Traffic Light Study Guide

Section	Page	I can …	Red	Yellow	Green
1.7	82 - 83	Define *reaction mechanism*, *elementary process*, and *molecularity (unimolecular, bimolecular, and termolecular steps).*	○	○	○
	83, 86	Define a *reaction intermediate* and identify the reaction intermediate(s) in a reaction mechanism.	○	○	○
	83 - 86	Identify a catalyst in a reaction mechanism and illustrate how a catalyst may affect a reaction's potential energy diagram.	○	○	○
	82 - 86	Algebraically sum the elementary processes in a reaction mechanism to provide the overall reaction.	○	○	○
	84 - 85	Describe and explain the concept of a *rate-determining step*. Cite four factors that could be responsible for a step being the rate-determining step in a mechanism.	○	○	○
	87 - 88	Define *heterogeneous catalysis* and *homogeneous catalysis* and give an example of each.	○	○	○
	88 - 91	Determine the rate law of a reaction from its mechanism.	○	○	○

For more support in AP Chemistry 2, go to edvantagescience.com

1.1 Measuring the Rate of Chemical Reactions

1. Give three reasons why the distance-time data in the Warm Up at the beginning of this section is so different from the property-time data collected for a typical chemical reaction.

2. Consider the following reaction, which could be done in either flask, using any of the equipment shown:

$6\ Cu(s) + 8\ HNO_3(aq) + O_2(g) \rightarrow 6\ CuNO_3(aq) + 4\ H_2O(l) + 2\ NO_2(g)$

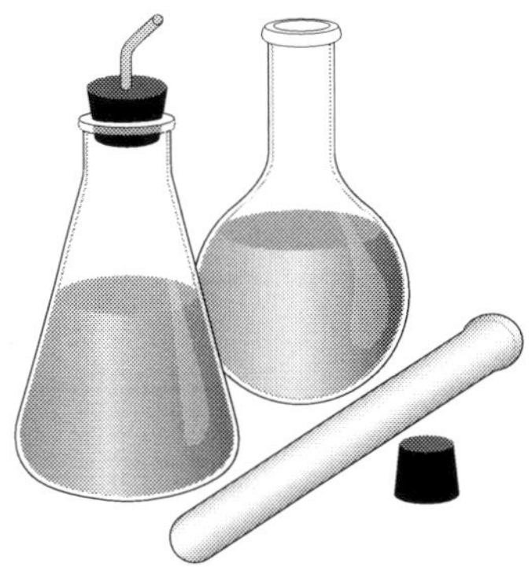

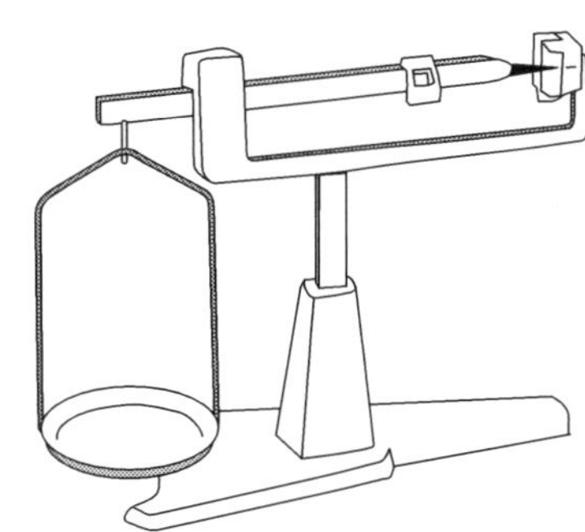

(a) If 5.00 g of copper solid is completely reacted in 250.0 mL of excess nitric acid in 7.00 min at STP, calculate the rate of the reaction in:

(i) g Cu/min

(ii) g NO_2/min

(iii) mol HNO_3/min

(b) Assume the reaction continues at this average rate for 10.0 min total time. Determine the final:

(i) mL NO_2 formed at STP

(ii) molarity of $CuNO_3$

(c) Describe SIX ways you might measure the reaction rate. Include the equipment required, measurements made and units for the rate. You may use a labeled diagram.

3. Consider the graph for the following reaction:
$CaCO_3(s) + 2\ HCl(aq) \rightarrow CaCl_2(aq) + CO_2(g) + H_2O(l)$

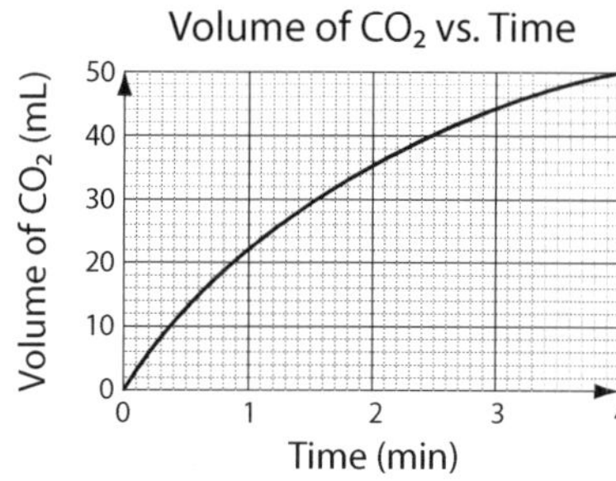

Recall the discussion of the *instantaneous rate* earlier in this section.

(a) Determine the instantaneous rate at the following times:
(i) an instant after 0 min (This is the *initial rate*.)

(ii) 1 min

(iv) 4 min

(b) How do these rates compare? What do you suppose causes this pattern?

4. Here is a table indicating the volume of gas collected as a disk of strontium metal reacts in a solution of hydrochloric acid for 1 min.
$Sr(s) + 2\ HCl(aq) \rightarrow SrCl_2(aq) + H_2(g)$

Time (seconds)	Volume of Hydrogen at STP (mL)
0	0
10.0	22.0
20.0	40.0
30.0	55.0
40.0	65.0
50.0	72.0
60.0	72.0

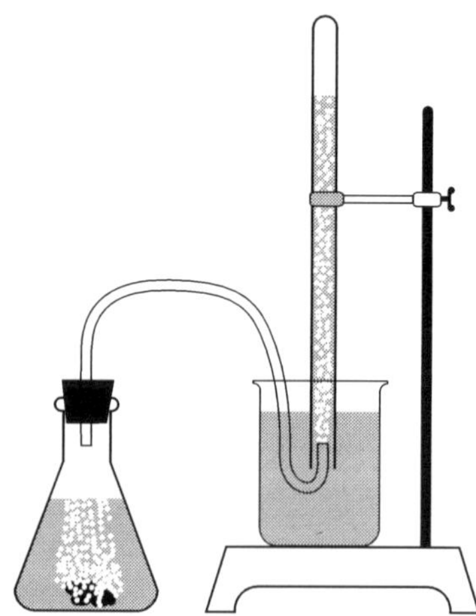

(a) Calculate the average rate of reaction in moles of HCl consumed/second over the first 50.0 s.

(b) Calculate the mass of strontium consumed in this 50.0 s period.

(c) Why did the volume of gas collected decrease in each increment until 50.0 s?

(d) Why did the volume of gas remain unchanged from 50.0 s to 60.0 s?

5. The spectrophotometer works by shining a single wavelength of light through a sample of a colored solution. A photocell detects the amount of light that passes through the solution as **% transmittance** and the amount of light that does not pass through as the **absorbance**. The more concentrated the solution, the darker the color. Dark color leads to a lower percentage of light transmitted and thus a higher absorbance. There is a direct relationship between absorbance and the concentration of a colored solution. The "calibration curve" (actually a straight line) below was created using solutions of *known* $Cu(NO_3)_2$ concentration.

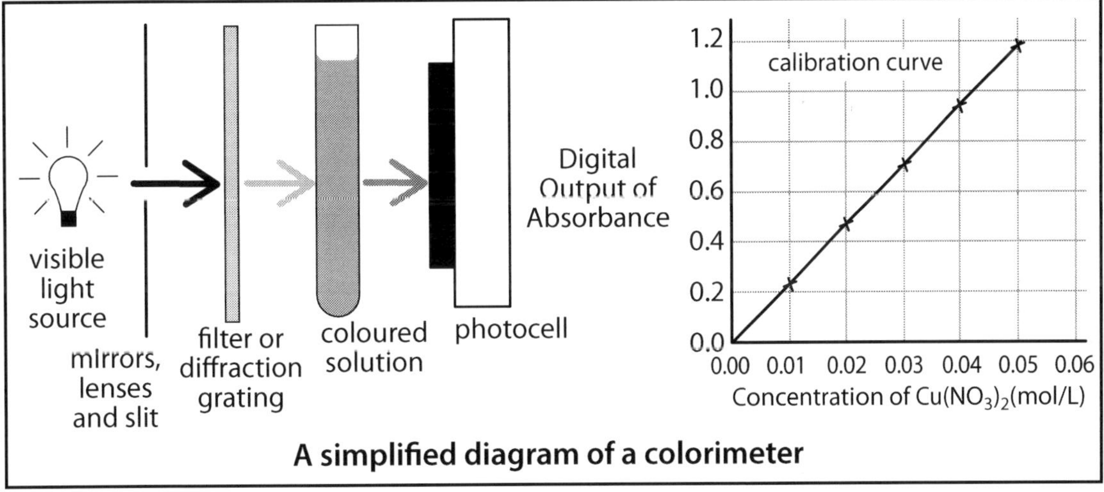

A simplified diagram of a colorimeter

A copper sample was reacted with 250 mL of nitric acid by the following reaction:

$3\ Cu(s) + 8\ HNO_3(aq) \rightarrow 3\ Cu(NO_3)_2(aq) + 2\ NO(g) + 4\ H_2O(l)$

As the reaction proceeded, small aliquots were removed and placed in a cuvette (the special test tube used to hold a sample in the spectrophotometer). The cuvettes were then placed in the instrument and the absorbances were recorded as follows:

Time (seconds)	Absorbances (no unit)	Concentration of Copper(II) Ion (mol/L)
0	0	0 mol/L
20.	0.40	
40.	0.70	
60.	0.90	
80.	1.00	

Find the absorbances on the standard graph and record the corresponding concentrations of the copper(II) ions (equal to the concentration of $Cu(NO_3)_2$) in the table.

(a) Calculate the average rate of the reaction from time 0 s to 80. s in units of M of $HNO_3(aq)$/s.

(b) What mass of Cu(*s*) will be consumed during the 80. s trial?

(c) What will you observe in the main reaction flask as the reaction proceeds?

1.1 Activity: Summarizing a Concept in Kinetics

Question

How can you summarize the methods that are useful for measuring the rate of a chemical reaction?

Background

As you're moving through any course in senior high school or university, it is very useful to summarize the concepts you learn into "chunks" of material. These summary notes may take the form of bulleted points or tables or charts.

Procedure

1. Use the outline provided below to organize what you've learned about methods that are useful for measuring the rates of various chemical reactions.
2. For each method, provide a balanced chemical equation for a reaction that could be measured using that method. Do not repeat equations that were already used in this section of the book. Your textbook and the Internet may be helpful for finding examples if you're having trouble recalling the major reaction types.
3. The first row has been completed as an example of what is expected. Note that the same property may be used multiple times (for example, with different states of species).

Property	State of Species	Apparatus Used	Units	Sample Reaction
Mass	solid	balance	g/min	$2\ K(s) + 2\ H_2O(l) \rightarrow 2\ KOH(aq) + H_2(g)$
Mass	gas			
Volume				
Concentration				
pH				
Color				
Pressure				
Conductivity				

Results and Discussion

1. You will find it extremely helpful to produce similar formats to help you summarize material for study in the remaining sections of this course. Dedicate a section of your notebook for these summary notes and refer to them from time to time to help you prepare for your unit and final examinations.

1.2 Factors Affecting Rates of Reaction

1. Identify the four factors that affect the rate of any reaction. Give a brief explanation as to how each one applies. Which of these factors can be altered to change the rate of a particular chemical reaction?

2. Identify the one factor that affects only the rate of heterogeneous reactions. Explain why it does not affect homogeneous reaction rates.

3. Use the Internet to find examples of catalysts that do the following:
   (a) Convert oxides of nitrogen into harmless nitrogen gas in the catalytic converter of an automobile.
   (b) Increase the rate of the Haber process to make ammonia.
   (c) Found on disinfectant discs to clean contact lenses.
   (d) Found in green plants to assist in photosynthesis.

4. How would each of the following changes affect the rate of decomposition of a marble statue due to acid rain? Begin by writing the equation for the reaction between marble (calcium carbonate) and nitric acid below.
   (a) The concentration of the acid is increased.
   (b) Erosion due to wind and weathering increases the surface area on the surface of the statue.
   (c) The statue is cooled in cold winter weather.
   (d) The partial pressure of carbon dioxide gas in the atmosphere is increased due to greenhouse gases.

5. (a) At room temperature, catalyzed decomposition of methanoic acid, HCOOH, produced 80.0 mL of carbon monoxide gas in 1.00 min once the volume was adjusted to STP conditions. The other product was water. Calculate the average rate of decomposition of methanoic acid in moles per minute.

(b) Give general (approximate) answers for the following:

(i) How long would you expect the production of 40.0 mL of gas to take?

(ii) How long would you expect the production of 80.0 mL to take without a catalyst?

(iii) How long would you expect the production of 80.0 mL of gas to take at 10°C above the experimental conditions?

6. Answer the questions below for each of the following reactions:

(i) $C(s) + O_2(g) \rightarrow CO_2(g)$

(ii) $Pb^{2+}(aq) + 2\,I^-(aq) \rightarrow PbI_2(s)$

(iii) $Mg(s) + CuCl_2(aq) \rightarrow MgCl_2(aq) + Cu(s)$

(a) Indicate whether you think it would be fast or slow if performed at room temperature. Then rank the three reactions from fastest to slowest.

(b) List which of the five factors could be used to increase the rate of each reaction.

7. Rank the diagrams below in order of expected reaction rate for this reaction:
$G(g) + B(g) \rightarrow GB(g)$
where G = gray, B = black and GB is the product. Explain your ranking. Assume the same temperature in all three reacting systems.

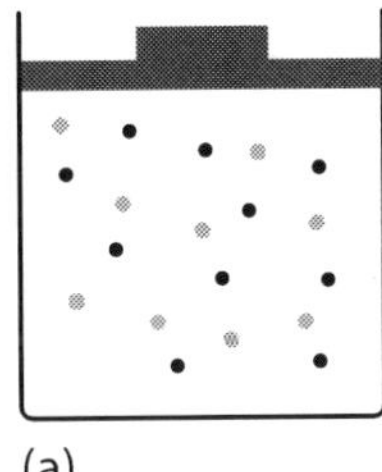

(a)

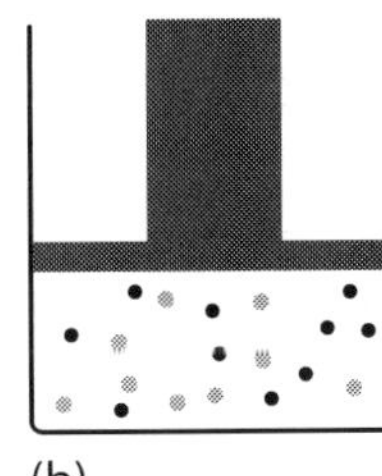

(b)

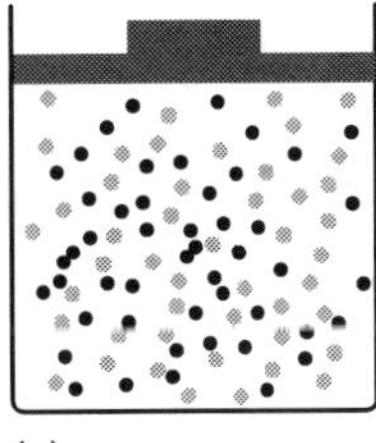

(c)

1.2 Activity: Graphic Depiction of Factors Affecting Reaction Rates

Question

How do concentration, surface area, and temperature affect reaction rate?

Background

Four trials were carried out in which a chunk of zinc was reacted with hydrochloric acid under four different sets of conditions. In all four trials, the chunk of zinc was of equal mass. The data collected indicate that varying factors have a significant impact on reaction rate. These data can be represented in tabular and graphical form.

The reaction was allowed to proceed for the same time period in each trial. In all four trials, the gas was collected in a eudiometer using the apparatus shown below.

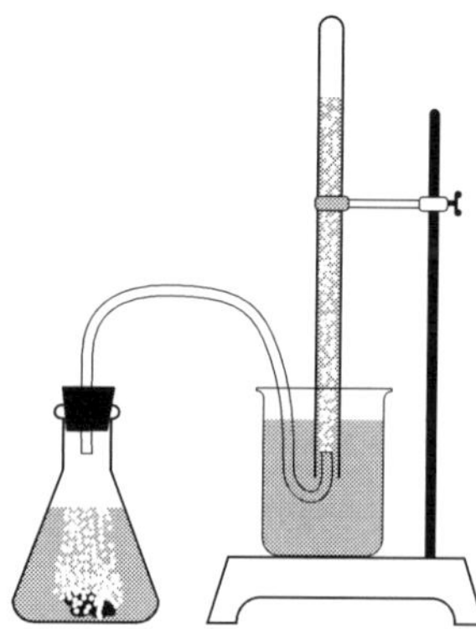

Time (s)	Trial 1 25°C, 1 M HCl (mL)	Trial 2 50°C, 1 M HCl (mL)	Trial 3 25°C, 2 M HCl (mL)	Trial 4 25°C, 1 M HCl, zinc powder (mL)
0	0	0	0	0
30.	12	34	20	26
60.	19	56	34	44
90.	24	65	44	57
120.	27	65	51	65
150.	29	65	54	65

Procedure

1. Use the following grid to graph all four sets of data. Vary colors for each trial line.

Results and Discussion

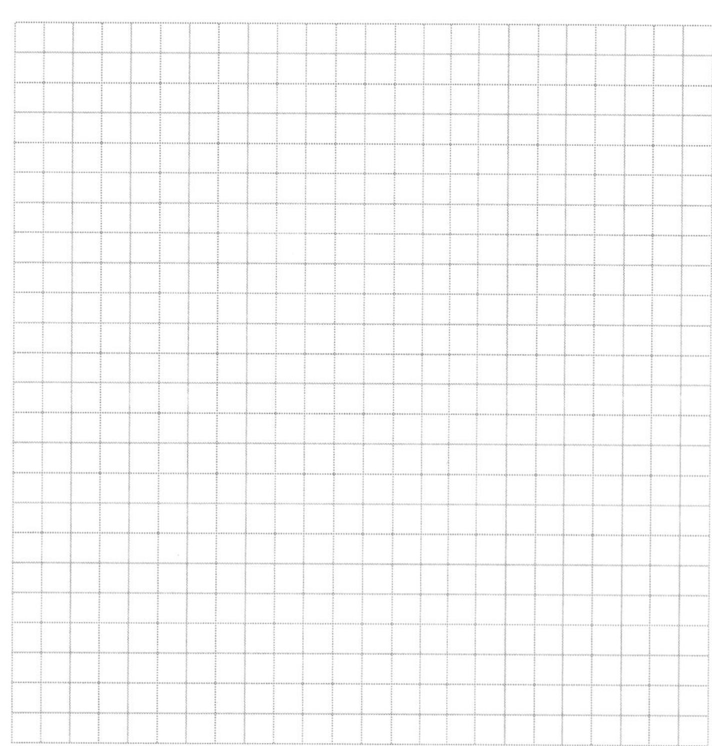

1. Write a balanced equation for the reaction that was studied.

2. Rank the conditions from those producing the fastest to slowest reaction rates. What factor influences reaction rate the most? Which factor is second most effective? Which factor has the least influence on the rate?

3. Calculate the average reaction rate in mL H_2/min for each trial. Use the time required to collect the maximum amount of hydrogen gas formed (e.g., the time for trial 2 will be 90. s). Place the rates on the graphed lines.

4. How many milligrams of zinc were used in 1.50 min for each trial? Assume a molar volume for $H_2(g)$ of 24.5 L/mol. (This is for SATP conditions or 25°C and 101.3 kPa or the pressure at sea level.) For the 50°C trial, use 26.5 L/mol.

5. What error is introduced by the assumption in question 4? Would the actual mass of Zn be larger or smaller than that calculated? Explain.

1.3 Collision Theory

1. List the two things that affect the rates of all chemical reactions according to collision theory.

2. What are the two requirements for a collision to be successful?

3. One chunk of zinc is left whole and another is cut into pieces as shown. Both samples of zinc are reacted in an equal volume of 6.0 mol/L aqueous hydrochloric acid.

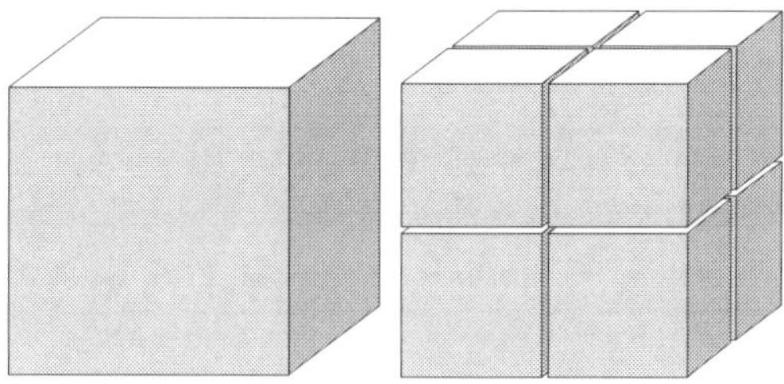

(a) Assuming the surface area of the first zinc sample is 6.00 cm^2, what is the surface area of the second sample of zinc?

(b) Compare the frequency of collisions between the hydrochloric acid and the single piece of zinc with those between the acid and the cut sample of zinc.

(c) Assuming the average rate of reaction for the single piece of zinc with the acid is 1.20×10^{-3} mol Zn/min, calculate the rate of reaction for the cut sample of zinc.

(d) Assuming this rate is maintained for a period of 4.50 min, how many milliliters of hydrogen gas would be collected at STP?

4. A reaction between ammonium ions and nitrite ions has the following rate law:

$$\text{rate} = k[NH_4^+][NO_2^-]$$

Assume the rate of formation of the salt is 3.10×10^{-3} mol/L/s. Note that the units may also be expressed as mol/L s. The reaction is performed in aqueous solution at room temperature.

(a) What rate of reaction would result if the $[NH_4^+]$ was tripled and the $[NO_2^-]$ was halved?

(b) Determine the reaction rate if the $[NH_4^+]$ was unchanged and the $[NO_2^-]$ was increased by a factor of four?

(c) If the $[NH_4^+]$ and the $[NO_2^-]$ were unchanged, but the rate increased to 6.40×10^{-3} mol/L s, what must have happened to the reacting system?

(d) What would the new reaction rate be if enough water were added to double the overall volume?

5. A student reacts ground marble chips, $CaCO_3(s)$, with hydrochloric acid, $HCl(aq)$, in an open beaker at constant temperature.

(a) In terms of collision theory, explain what will happen to the rate of the reaction as it proceeds from the beginning to completion.

(b) Sketch a graph of volume of $CO_2(g)$ vs. time to show the formation of product with time as the reaction proceeds.

6. Consider the following three experiments, each involving the same mass of zinc and the same volume of acid at the same temperature. Rank the three in order from fastest to slowest, and explain your ranking using collision theory.

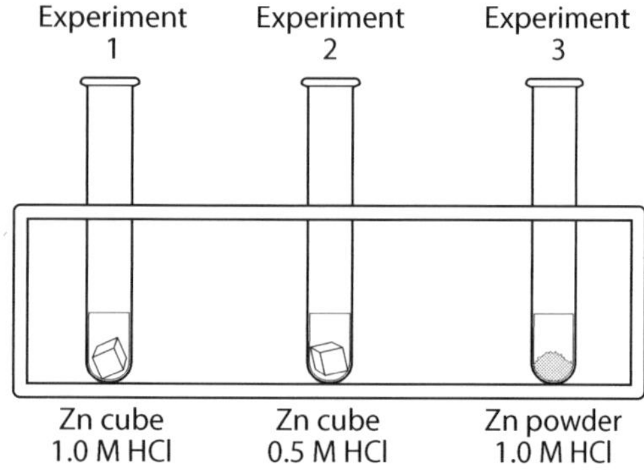

7. Is the following collision likely to produce Cl_2 and NO_2 assuming the collision occurs with sufficient energy? If not, redraw the particles in such a way that a successful collision would be likely.

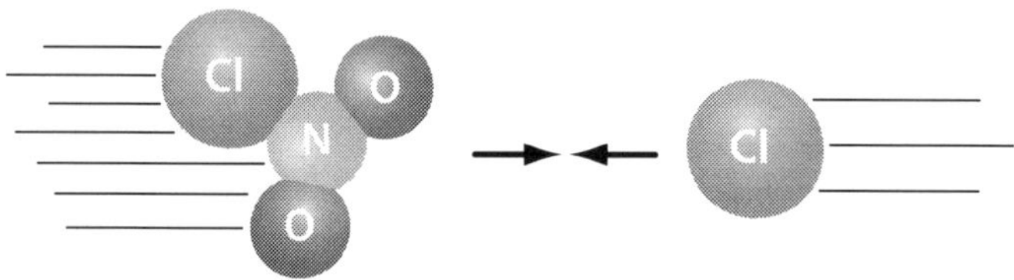

8. Use collision theory to explain each of the following.
   (a) Food found in camps half way up Mount Everest is still edible once thawed.

   (b) Campers react magnesium shavings with oxygen to start fires.

   (c) A thin layer of platinum in a vehicle's exhaust system converts oxides of nitrogen into non-toxic nitrogen gas.

1.3 Activity: Tracking a Collision

Question

How is a single reactant particle affected by a variety of factors that impact the rate of a chemical reaction?

Background

A variety of factors may affect the rate of a chemical reaction. These factors include the nature of the reactants, the concentration of the reactants, their surface area, temperature, and the presence of a catalyst.

Procedure

1. The diagrams below represent snapshots taken within a nanosecond of the "life" of an ordinary gas particle. None of these particles reacts during this time, but they do a lot of colliding. Follow the pathway of an individual reactant particle as several of the factors affecting reaction rates are changed. Each time the particle changes direction it has collided with either another particle or the walls of the container.
2. While the temperature remains constant, the concentration of the reacting particle is doubled in each frame from (a) to (b) to (c).

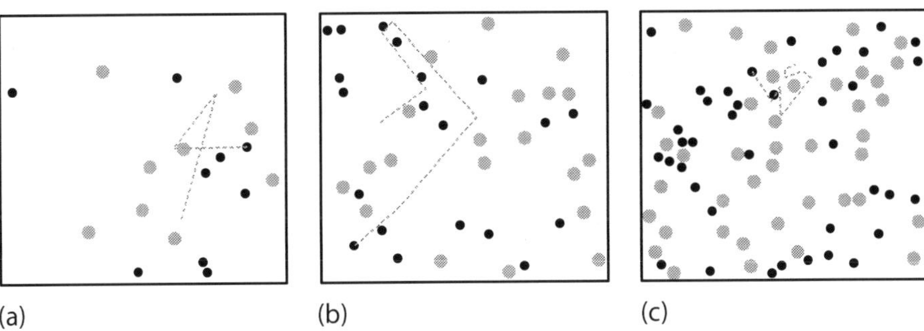

3. The temperature of the reaction system is increased from 25°C to 35°C to 45°C.

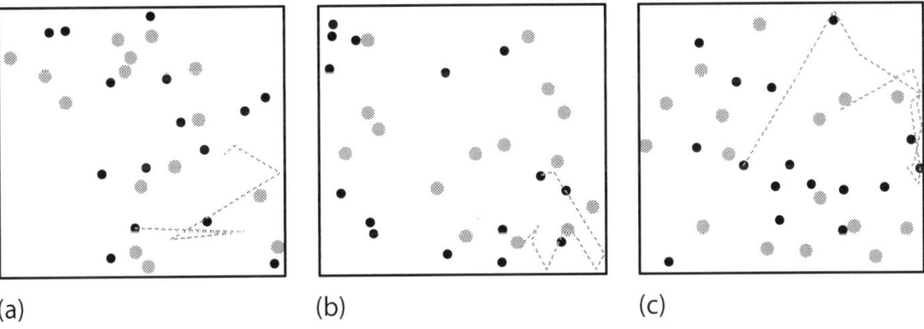

4. The volume of the reaction system is decreased by approximately half from (a) to (b) and again to (c), causing the pressure to approximately double each time. Assume the temperature remains constant.

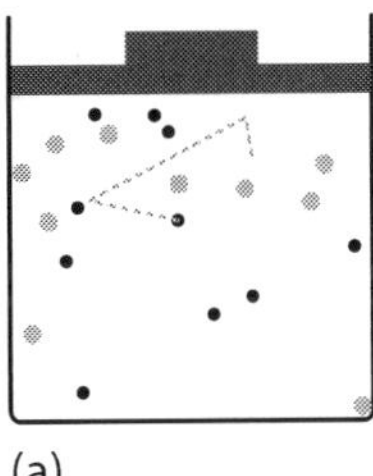
(a)

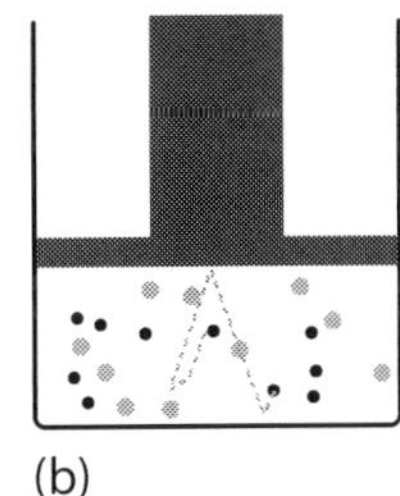
(b)

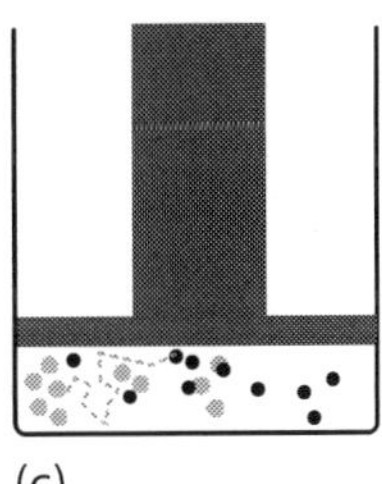
(c)

Results and Discussion

1. Complete the following table by indicating the number of collisions experienced by each reacting particle.

The Number of Collisions per Unit of Time	Snapshot (a)	Snapshot (b)	Snapshot (c)
Snapshot series 1 (effect of concentration)			
Snapshot series 2 (effect of temperature)			
Snapshot series 3 (effect of volume/pressure)			

2. Which two of the three factors shown produce the most similar effect on the rate of a chemical reaction?

3. One of the three factors will increase reaction rate more than the other two. Which factor is this?

4. Why would this factor have more of an impact on reaction rate than the other two?

5. Reaction rates are increased by collisions occurring more frequently and by collisions occurring more effectively. Which of these two things would be impacted by:
   (a) the addition of a catalyst to a reaction system?

   (b) increasing the surface area in a heterogeneous reaction?

1.4 Determining Rate Laws from Experimental Data

1. Consider the hypothetical reaction: X + Y → Z and the following data:

Initial Rate of Appearance of Z (mol/L/s)	$[X]_0$ (mol/L)	$[Y]_0$ (mol/L)
0.053	0.05	0.25
0.127	0.10	0.15
1.02	0.20	0.30
0.254	0.10	0.30
0.509	0.20	0.15

(a) Use the data in the table to determine the rate law for the reaction.

(b) Determine the value of the rate constant with units.

(c) Determine the initial rate of appearance of Z when the concentration of X is 0.15 mol/L and that of Y is 0.20 mol/L.

2. Nitrosyl fluoride, NO_2F, can be made by reacting NO_2 and F_2 gases as follows:

$$2\ NO_2(g) + F_2(g) \rightarrow 2\ NO_2F(g)$$

The following table represents data collected for the rate of formation of nitrosyl fluoride at room temperature. Recall that mol L^{-1} is equivalent to mol/L.

$[NO_2]_0$ (mol·L^{-1})	$[F_2]_0$ (mol·L^{-1})	Rate (mol·L^{-1}·s^{-1})
0.00100	0.00100	4.00×10^{-5}
0.00100	0.00300	1.20×10^{-4}
0.00500	0.00300	6.00×10^{-4}
0.00500	0.00500	1.00×10^{-3}

(a) Use the data in the table to determine the rate law for the reaction.

(b) Calculate the rate constant at room temperature. Include appropriate units.

3. The following trials were performed during the kinetic study of an oxidation-reduction reaction:

$$2\ MnO_4^-(aq) + 5\ H_2C_2O_4(aq) + 6\ H^+(aq) \rightarrow 2\ Mn^{2+}(aq) + 10\ CO_2(g) + 8\ H_2O(l)$$

$[MnO_4^-]_{initial}$ (mol/L)	$[H_2C_2O_4]_{initial}$(mol/L)	$[H^+]_{initial}$ (mol/L)	Initial Rate of Formation of Mn^{2+} (mol/L/s)
1.0×10^{-3}	1.0×10^{-3}	1.0	2.0×10^{-4}
2.0×10^{-3}	1.0×10^{-3}	1.0	8.0×10^{-4}
2.0×10^{-3}	2.0×10^{-3}	1.0	1.6×10^{-3}
2.0×10^{-3}	2.0×10^{-3}	2.0	1.6×10^{-3}

(a) Use the data in the table for the initial rates of formation of the manganese(II) ion to determine the rate law and the rate constant for the redox reaction.

(b) By what factor would the initial reaction rate change if the concentrations of all three reactants doubled?

(c) By what factor would the initial reaction rate change if the volume of the reaction system doubled due to the addition of distilled water?

4. The equation for a general reaction is: $2\ A(g) + 2\ B(g) \rightarrow C(g) + 2\ D(g)$. The initial rate of formation of C is determined in four trials with various initial concentrations of reactants as shown in the table.

Trial Number	Initial [A] ($mol \cdot L^{-1}$)	Initial [B] ($mol \cdot L^{-1}$)	Initial Reaction Rate ($mol \cdot L^{-1} \cdot s^{-1}$)
1	0.100	0.100	4.00×10^{-5}
2	0.200	0.100	1.60×10^{-4}
3	0.100	0.200	4.00×10^{-5}
4	0.300	0.200	?

(a) Determine the rate law for the reaction.

(b) Determine the rate constant with units.

(c) Calculate the initial reaction rate for Trial 4.

5. The table below provides data obtained under lab conditions for the reaction:

$$2\ MnO_4^{2-} + H_3IO_6^{2-} \rightarrow 2\ MnO_4^- + IO_3^- + 3\ OH^-$$

The experimental trials involved measuring the initial rate of formation of the iodate (IO_3^-) ion with varying initial concentrations of reactants.

Experimental Trial	$[MnO_4^{2-}]_0$ (mol·L^{-1})	$[H_3IO_6^{2-}]_0$ (mol·L^{-1})	Initial Rate (*M*/min)
1	1.6×10^{-4}	3.1×10^{-4}	2.6×10^{-6}
2	6.4×10^{-4}	3.1×10^{-4}	4.2×10^{-5}
3	1.6×10^{-4}	6.2×10^{-4}	2.6×10^{-6}
4	3.2×10^{-4}	3.1×10^{-4}	?
5	?	6.2×10^{-4}	2.3×10^{-5}

(a) Determine the rate law for the reaction.

(b) Calculate the rate constant with units.

(c) What is the initial rate of formation of IO_3^- ion for Trial 4?

(d) What is the required initial concentration of MnO_4^{2-} ion for Trial 5?

(e) What is the initial rate of formation of MnO_4^- ion for Trial 1?

6. The equation for the bromination of acetone in acidic solution is:

$$CH_3COCH_3(aq) + Br_2(aq) \rightarrow CH_3COCH_2Br(aq) + H^+(aq) + Br^-(aq)$$

The following data were collected in four trials by varying the concentration of reactants and measuring the initial rate of disappearance of aqueous bromine ($Br_2(aq)$).

Trial Number	$[CH_3COCH_3]_0$ (*M*)	$[Br_2]_0$ (*M*)	$[H^+]_0$ (*M*)	Initial Rate (*M*/s)
1	0.30	0.050	0.050	5.7×10^{-5}
2	0.30	0.100	0.050	5.7×10^{-5}
3	0.30	0.100	0.100	1.4×10^{-4}
4	0.40	0.050	0.200	3.2×10^{-4}

Determine the rate law and the rate constant (with appropriate units) for the acidic bromination of acetone.

1.5 Integrated Rate Equations

1. (a) What happens to each of the following as time passes for a first-order reaction?
   (i) rate of reaction

   (ii) rate constant

   (iii) half-life

   (b) Answer question (a) for a zero-order reaction.
   (i) rate of reaction

   (ii) rate constant

   (iii) half-life

   (c) Answer question (a) for a second-order reaction.
   (i) rate of reaction

   (ii) rate constant

   (iii) half-life

2. The rate constant of a first-order reaction is $4.03 \times 10^{-3}\ s^{-1}$. What concentration of reactant remains after 74.6 s assuming an initial concentration of 0.300 mol/L?

3. The reaction $2\ B \rightarrow C + A$ is a second-order reaction, and the rate constant is 0.15 L/mol·min. If the initial concentration of B is 2.00 mol/L, what is the concentration of B after 45 min?

4. A zero-order reaction has $k = 0.0025$ mol/L/s for the disappearance of A. What is the concentration of A after 35 s if the initial concentration is 0.50 mol/L?

5. In 17.5% w/w HCl, the complex ion $Ru(NH_3)_6^{3+}$ decomposes to a variety of products. The reaction is first order in $[Ru(NH_3)_6^{3+}]$ and has a half-life of 14 h at 25°C.
   (a) What is the rate constant for this reaction?

   (b) Under these conditions, how long will it take for the $[Ru(NH_3)_6^{3+}]$ to decrease to 6.25% of its initial value?

6. What is the rate constant in s^{-1} for a first-order reaction with an initial concentration of 0.600 mol/L if, after 142 s, the concentration is 0.444 mol/L?

7. What is the half-life in seconds for a second-order reaction with the rate constant $k = 2.74 \times 10^{-1}$ L $mol^{-1}s^{-1}$ if the initial reactant concentration is 0.500 mol/L?

8. Compare the two graphs shown here, focusing on lines (a), (b), and (c), which represent plots for various experimental trials run for the same first-order reaction under different conditions.

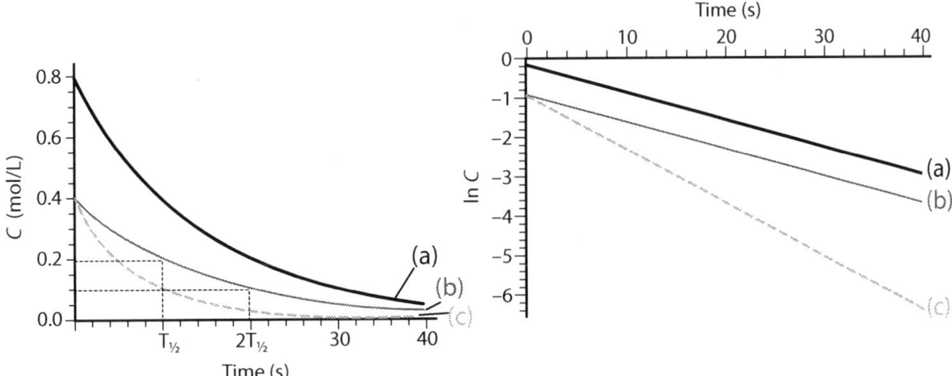

(a) What condition was changed from trial (a) to trial (b)?

(b) What effect did the change have? Explain your answer.

(c) What was not affected by the change? Justify your answer.

(d) What condition was changed from trial (b) to trial (c)? Be specific.

(e) Give two things about the reaction that this change impacted. Justify your answers.

9. Compare the two graphs shown here, focusing on lines (a), (b), and (c), which represent plots for the same second-order reaction under different conditions.

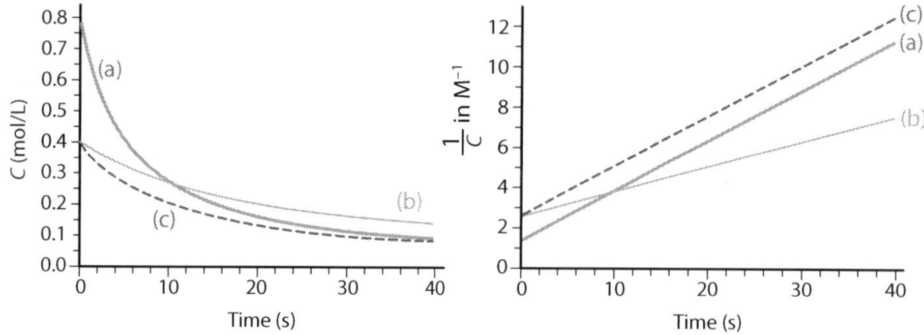

(a) What condition was changed from trial (a) to trial (b)?

(b) What effect did the change have? Explain your answer.

(c) What was not affected by the change? Justify your answer.

(d) What condition was changed from trial (b) to trial (c)? Be specific.

(e) Give two effects the change had on the reaction? Justify your answers.

10. The decomposition of aqueous sucrose to form the isomers glucose and fructose is a common organic reaction, which requires a strong acid catalyst: $C_{12}H_{22}O_{11}(aq) + H_2O(l) \rightarrow 2\ C_6H_{12}O_6(aq)$. The following data were collected during the process:

Time (min)	$[C_{12}H_{22}O_{11}]$ (mol/L)
0	0.316
39	0.274
80	0.238
140	0.190
210	0.146

Use the following grids to plot three separate graphs of $[C_{12}H_{22}O_{11}]$, ln $[C_{12}H_{22}O_{11}]$, and 1/$[C_{12}H_{22}O_{11}]$ against time to determine the reaction order.

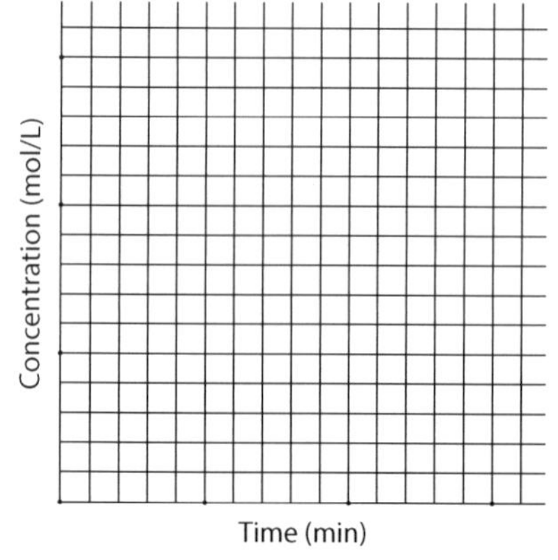

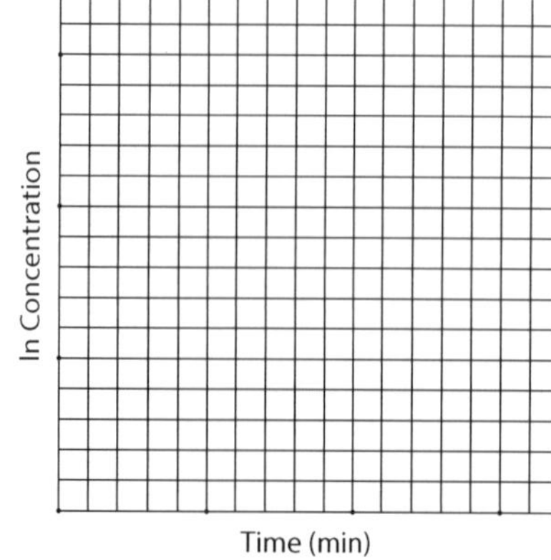

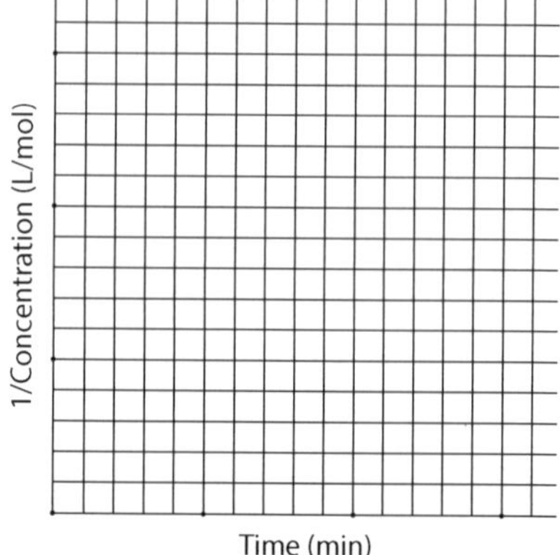

(a) Write the rate law expression in its general form (water should not be included).

(b) Determine the rate constant with units.

(c) Determine the half-life.

(d) If we performed a new trial with an initial concentration of sucrose of 0.400 mol/L, what concentration would remain after 4.00 h has passed?

11. Methyl isonitrile isomerizes to acetonitrile: $CH_3NC(g) \rightarrow CH_3CN(g)$ at 215°C.
The following data were collected during the process:

Time (s)	$[CH_3NC]$ (mol/L)
2000	0.0110
5000	0.0059
8000	0.0031
12000	0.0014
15000	0.0007

Use the following grids to plot three separate graphs of $[CH_3NC]$, ln $[CH_3NC]$, and $1/[CH_3NC]$ against time to determine the reaction order.

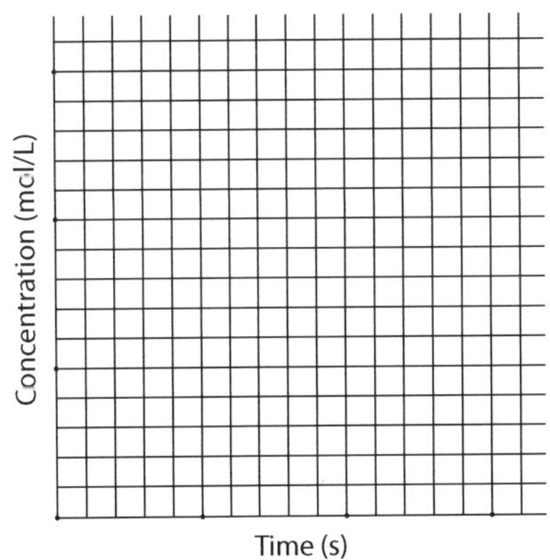

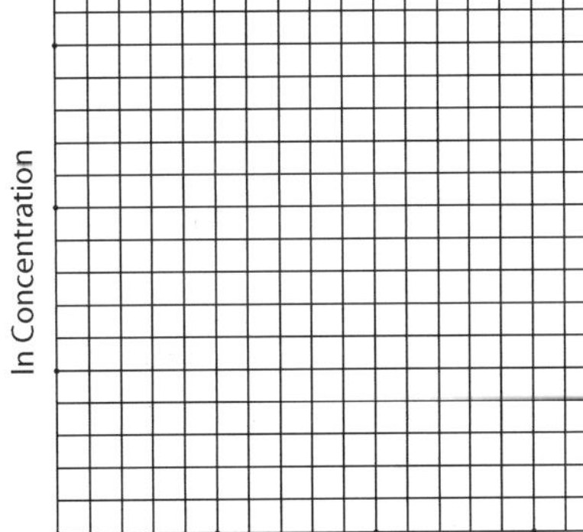

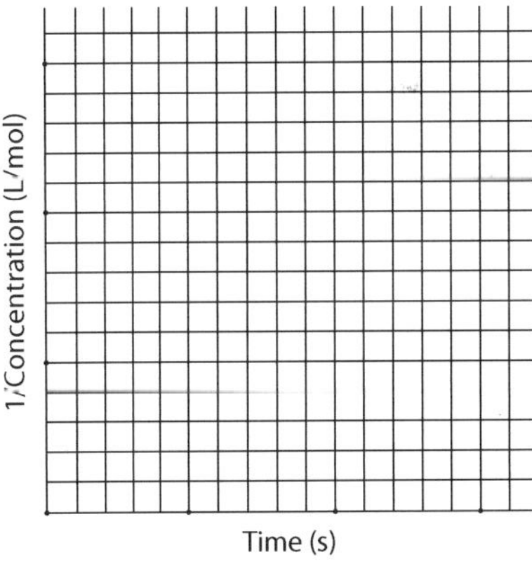

(a) Write the rate law expression in its general form.

(b) Determine the rate constant.

(c) Determine the half-life.

(d) Assuming the process continues, what concentration of methyl isonitrile would we expect after 5.00 h?

12. (a) What is the rate constant for a second-order reaction with an initial reactant concentration of 0.300 mol/L if after 158 s, the concentration is 0.200 mol/L?

(b) What is the half-life of this reaction?

13. Tritium decays by a first-order process that has a half-life of 12.5 y. How many years will it take to reduce the radioactivity of a tritium sample to 15% of its original value?

14. A zero-order reaction has a rate constant $k = 0.025$ mol/L/s for the disappearance of reactant, A.

(a) What is the half-life of this process?

(b) What will be the concentration of A after 15 s if the initial concentration is 0.50 mol/L?

15. The half-life is 22.7 s for the first-order conversion of cyclobutane to ethylene, $C_4H_8(g) \rightarrow 2\ C_2H_4(g)$, at a constant temperature. How much time, in seconds, does it take for the partial pressure of cyclobutane to decrease from 100.0 mmHg to 10.0 mmHg?

Table 1.5.1 *Summary of Integrated Rate Laws and Half-Lives*

Order in C	Rate Law	Integrated Form $y = mx + b$	Rate Constant (k) Units	Straight Line Plot	Half-life $t_{1/2}$	Graph
Zero order (n=0)	rate = $kC^0 = k$	$C_t = -kt + C_0$	$\frac{M}{s}$	C_t vs. t (slope = $-k$)	$t_{1/2} = \frac{C_0}{2k}$	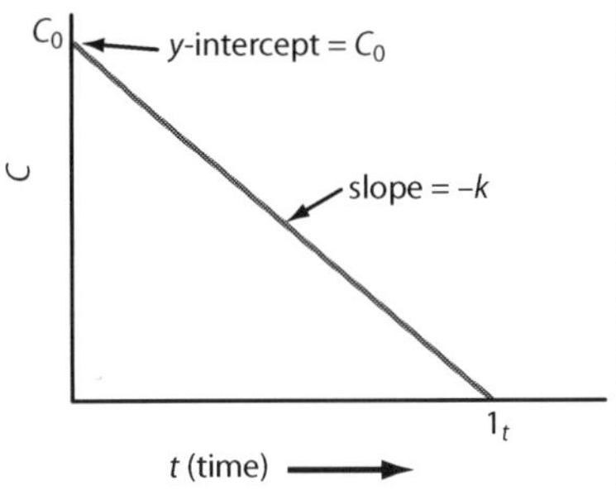 C; C_0 ← y-intercept = C_0; slope = $-k$; 1_t; t (time) →
First order (n=1)	rate = kC^1	$\ln C_t = -kt + \ln C_0$	$\frac{1}{s}$	$\ln C_t$ vs. t (slope = $-k$)	$t_{1/2} = \frac{\ln 2}{k} = \frac{0.693}{k}$	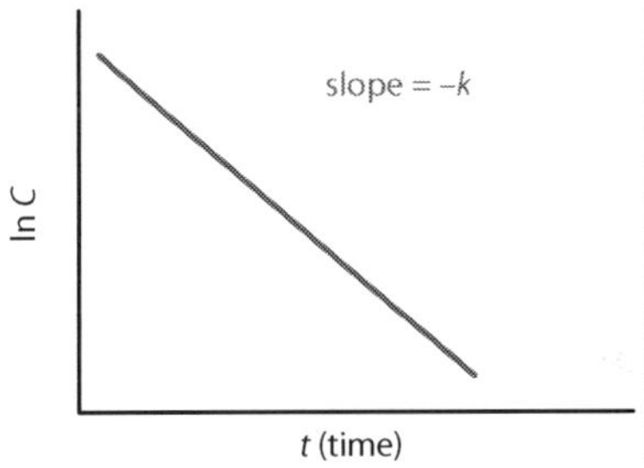 $\ln C$; slope = $-k$; t (time)
Second order (n=2)	rate = kC^2	$\frac{1}{C_t} = kt + \frac{1}{C_0}$	$\frac{1}{M \cdot s}$	$\frac{1}{C_t}$ vs. t (slope = k)	$t_{1/2} = \frac{1}{kC_0}$	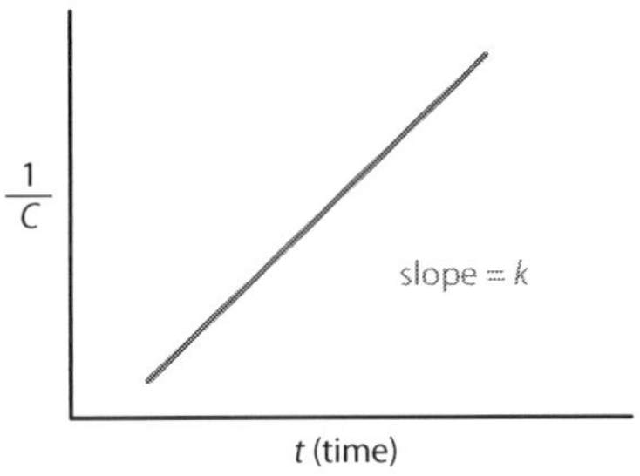 $\frac{1}{C}$; slope = k; t (time)
nth order	rate = kC^n	$\frac{1}{C^{(n-1)}} = (n-1)kt + \frac{1}{C_0^{(n-1)}}$	$\frac{1}{M^{(n-1)} \cdot s}$	$\frac{1}{C_t^{(n-1)}}$ vs. t (slope = $(n-1)k$)	$t_{1/2} = \frac{2^{(n-1)}-1}{(n-1)kC_0^{(n-1)}}$	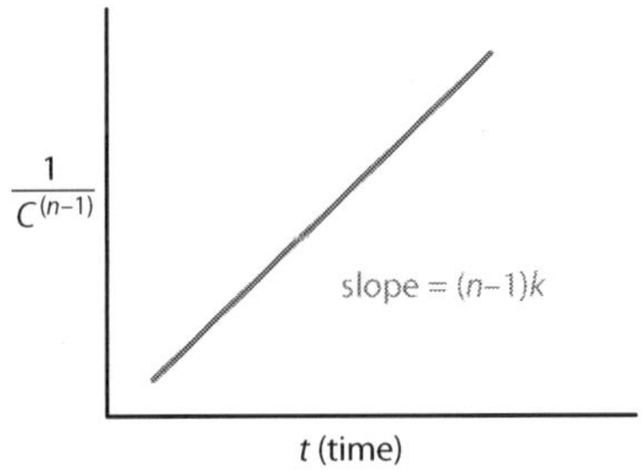 $\frac{1}{C^{(n-1)}}$; slope = $(n-1)k$; t (time)

1.6 Potential Energy Diagrams

1. Given the following ΔH values, write a balanced thermochemical equation and an equation using ΔH notation with the smallest possible whole number coefficients for each of the chemical changes given below.
   (a) The replacement of iron in thermite, $Fe_2O_3(s)$, by aluminum $\Delta H = -852$ kJ/molFe_2O_3

   (b) The formation of $Ca(OH)_2(s)$ from its elements $\Delta H = -986$ kJ/mol$Ca(OH)_2$

   (c) The decomposition of $H_2O(l)$ into its elements $\Delta H = +286$ kJ/molH_2O

2. Study the graphs shown below.
   (a) Draw a vertical line on the first graph to represent E_a. Place the line so that about 10% of the particles in the reacting sample have enough energy to react.
   (b) Rotate the first graph in such a way that the energy axes of the two graphs are both oriented up and down. Redraw the graph(s) in this orientation.
   (c) Explain what these graphs indicate about the reacting particles.

   (d) Repeat part (b) on the right side of the second graph.
   (e) What does this say about an endothermic reaction compared to an exothermic one?

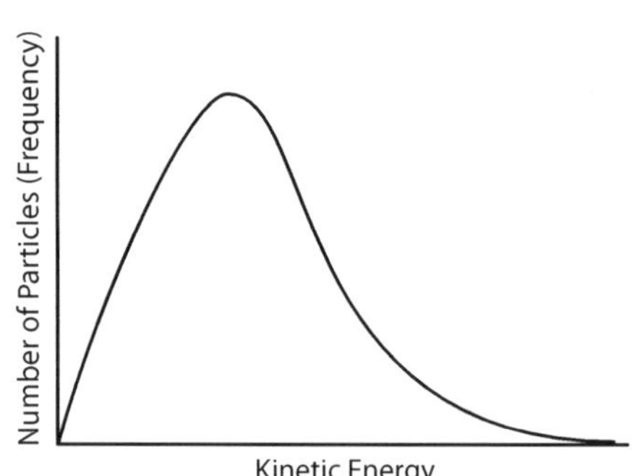

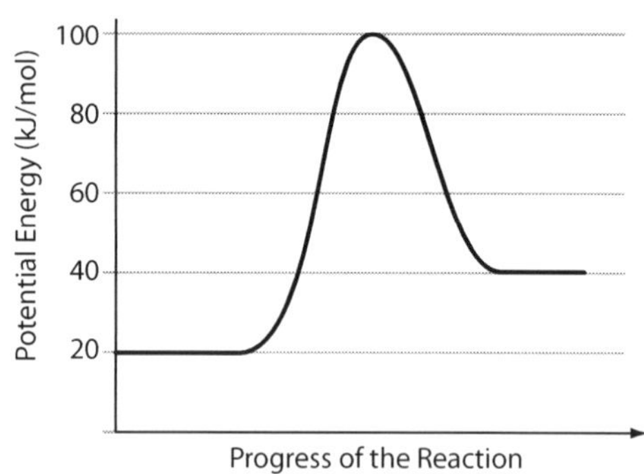

3. For a hypothetical reaction, $XY(g) \rightleftharpoons X(g) + Y(g)$ $\Delta H = 35$ kJ/mol. For the reverse reaction, $E_a = 25$ kJ/mol.
   (a) Sketch a potential energy diagram for this reaction (label general values as given).

   (b) What is the activation energy for the forward reaction?

   (c) What is ΔH for the reverse reaction?

4. Study the potential energy diagram shown below.

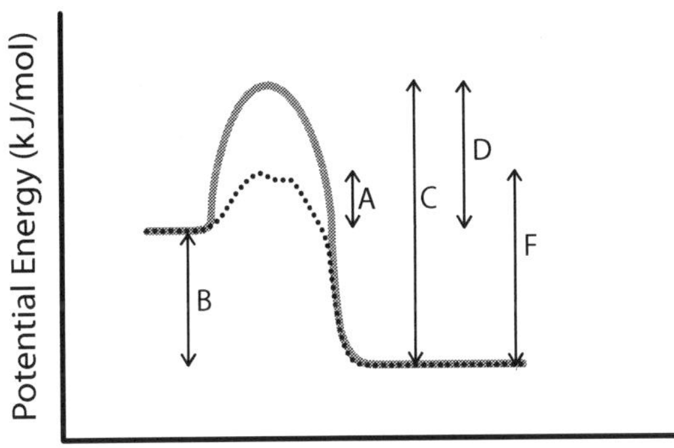

   (a) Indicate what each of the letters (A through E) represents.

   A.

   B.

   C.

   D.

   E.

   (b) Is this reaction endothermic or exothermic?

(c) How would the diagram be affected if the reacting system were heated?

5. Examine the following potential energy diagram for this reaction:

$Q + S \rightarrow T$

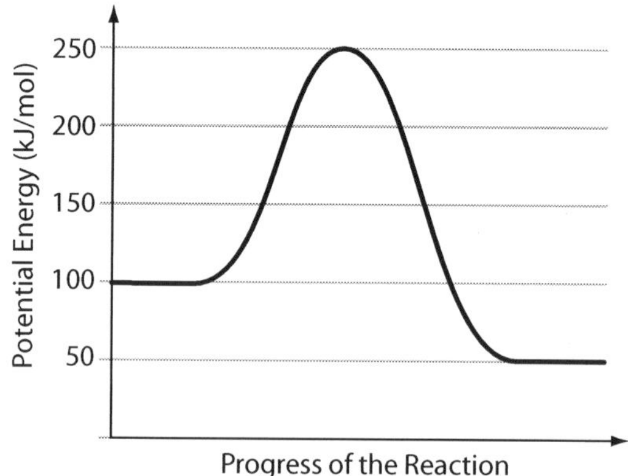

(a) Determine ΔH for the reaction.

(b) Write the thermochemical equation for the reaction.

(c) Rewrite the equation in ΔH notation.

(d) Classify the reaction as exothermic or endothermic.

(e) Determine the E_a of the reaction.

6. Why are exothermic reactions usually self-sustaining. In other words, why do they continue once supplied with activation energy? Use the burning of a pile of driftwood as an example.

7. Fill in the blanks for an EXOthermic reaction: The energy released during bond forming is ____________ than the energy required for bond ______________. As a result, there is a net _____________ of energy. The bonds formed have ____________ potential energy than the ______________ bonds did.

8. How would a PE diagram for a *fast* reaction compare to a PE diagram for a *slow* reaction? Explain.

9. (a) As two reactant particles approach one another for a collision, what happens to their kinetic energy? Why?

(b) What happens to their potential energy? Why?

(c) What happens to their total energy (sum of potential and kinetic)?

(d) Complete the following graph:

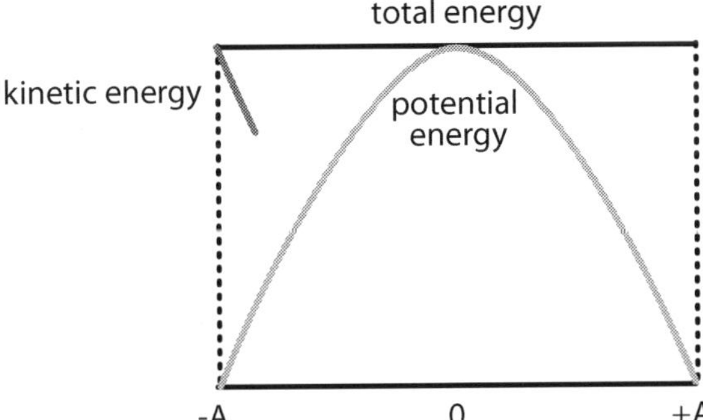

10. Study the following potential energy diagram.

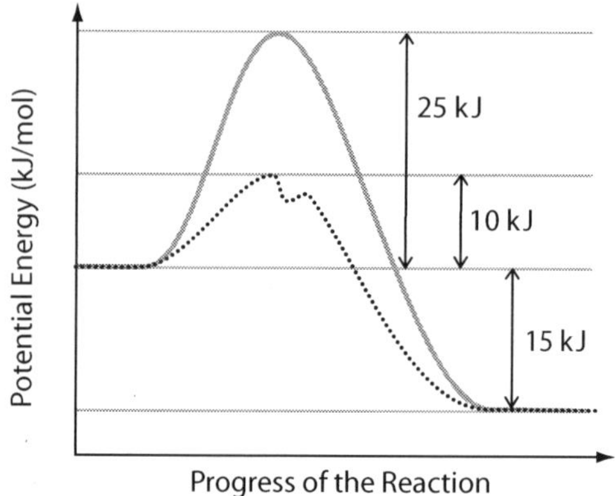

(a) Is this reaction endothermic or exothermic?

(b) What is E_a for the catalyzed pathway?

(c) What is E_a for the uncatalyzed pathway?

(d) What is ΔH for this reaction? How does this value change with a catalyst?

(e) How much lower is the potential energy of the activated complex with a catalyst?

(f) How does this affect the reaction rate?

1.6 Activity: Comparing and Contrasting Concepts in Kinetics

Question

How can you compare and contrast endothermic and exothermic processes?

Background

For this activity, you will use the method of "compare and contrast" to create a table that could become part of your summary notes for this section.

Procedure

1. Use the outline provided below to organize what you've learned about endothermic and exothermic reactions.
2. The first row has been completed as an example of what is expected. Note that there may be many other comparisons and contrasts (or similarities and differences) that you can add to your table. Don't feel limited to only those lines where clues have been provided.

Characteristic	Endothermic	Exothermic
Sensation	Feels cold	Feels hot
Sign of ΔH		
Change in enthalpy		
PE ← → KE transformation		
Sample thermochemical equation		
Sample equation using ΔH		
Bond energy comparisons		
Energy involved in breaking vs. forming bonds		
Sample PE diagram		

Results and Discussion

You will find it very helpful to produce similar charts to help you summarize material for study in the remaining sections of this course. Add these to the dedicated section of your notebook for summary notes and refer to them from time to time to help you in preparing for your unit and final examinations.

1.7 Reaction Mechanisms, Catalysis, and Rate Laws

1. What is a reaction mechanism?

2. What is a rate-determining step?

3. How do chemists determine reaction mechanisms?

4. Indicate whether each of the following reactions involves heterogeneous or homogeneous catalysis:

   (a) $H_2(g) + CH_2CH_2(g) \xrightarrow{Pt(s)} CH_3CH_3(g)$ hydrogenation of ethylene

   (b) Chlorofluorocarbons (CFCs) catalyze the conversion of ozone ($O_3(g)$) to oxygen gas (O_2).

   $2\,O_3(g) \xrightarrow{CFC(g)} 3\,O_2(g)$

   (c) Manganese(IV) oxide catalyzes the decomposition of hydrogen peroxide.

   $2\,H_2O_2(aq) \xrightarrow{MnO_2(s)} 2\,H_2O(l) + O_2(g)$

5. The oxygen produced by the decomposition of hydrogen peroxide may be used to clean a variety of items from contact lenses to dentures. The decomposition may be initiated by the addition of small disks. Study the following mechanism:

   1st: $H_2O_2(aq) + I^-(aq) \rightarrow H_2O(l) + IO^-(aq)$ slow

   2nd: $H_2O_2(aq) + IO^-(aq) \rightarrow H_2O(l) + O_2(g) + I^-(aq)$ fast

   Overall reaction:

   (a) Determine the overall reaction.

   (b) Identify any intermediate(s) present.

   (c) What is the material contained on the disks?

6. Examine the following potential energy diagram and use it to construct a reaction mechanism. Show each step and the overall reaction. Label the rate-determining step.

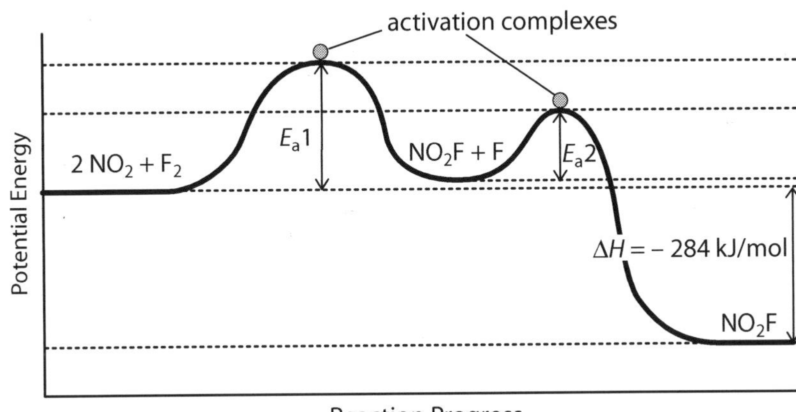

7. Look at the PE diagram shown here and answers the questions below. Write your answers at the end of each question.

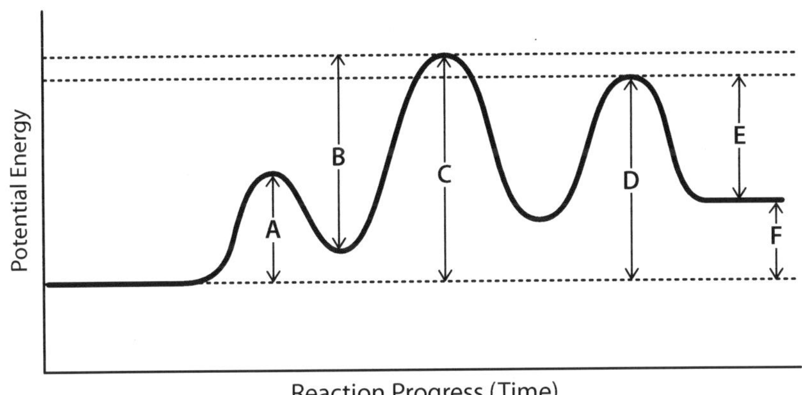

(a) How many steps are in the reaction represented by this potential energy profile?

(b) Which step is rate determining?

(c) What arrow represents E_a for the forward reaction?

(d) What arrow represents E_a for the rate-determining step?

(e) What arrow represents ΔH for the reaction?

(f) Is this an endo- or exothermic reaction?

8. The reaction, $CO(g) + NO_2(g) \rightarrow CO_2(g) + NO(g)$ may occur by either of the following two mechanisms:

Mechanism 1: Step 1: $2\,NO_2(g) \rightarrow NO_3(g) + NO(g)$ slow

Step 2: ____________________ fast

Reaction:

Mechanism 2: Step 1: $2\,NO_2(g) \rightarrow N_2O_4(g)$ fast

Step 2: ____________________ slow

Reaction:

(a) Fill the reaction in and use it to discern the missing step 2 for each mechanism.

(b) Experimental data shows that increasing the [CO] has *no effect* on the overall reaction rate. Based on this data, which mechanism must be correct?

9. Consider the reaction: $4\,HBr(g) + O_2(g) \rightarrow 2\,H_2O(g) + 2\,Br_2(g)$ + heat

(a) Does this reaction represent an elementary process? Explain

(b) Propose a reaction mechanism for the overall reaction, given the following clues: There are two intermediates in the reaction. The first to form is HOOBr(*g*) and the second is HOBr(*g*).

(c) Experimental data shows that a change in [HBr] has the same effect on the rate of the reaction as an identical change in $[O_2]$. What is the rate-determining step?

(d) Sketch a potential energy profile for the reaction. Recall that two identical steps involving the same potential bond energies will be shown as the *same step* in a potential energy diagram.

10. Sketch a potential energy diagram for the following reversible reaction:

$$\text{heat} + 2\,A + 2\,B \rightleftharpoons 3\,C$$

Be sure to label the axes. Indicate the following features on the diagram:

(a) reverse activation energy

(b) ΔH

(c) potential energy of activated complex

(d) use a dotted line to represent the pathway for a catalyzed reaction

11. Consider the following mechanism for a chemical reaction.

Step 1: $2\,NO(g) \rightleftharpoons N_2O_2(g)$ *fast-forward reversible*

Step 2: $N_2O_2(g) + O_2(g) \rightarrow 2\,NO_2(g)$ *slow*

(a) Determine the overall reaction. Indicate any catalysts or intermediates.

(b) Determine the rate law for the overall reaction.

12. A hypothetical reaction, $2\,A + B \rightarrow C + D$, has the rate law, rate = $k\,[A][B]$.
Your teacher proposes the following three reaction mechanisms for the reaction. Which of these mechanisms is consistent with the rate law ? Consider and address each mechanism in turn and justify your choice.

Mechanism 1: $A + B \rightleftharpoons C + M$ *fast-forward reversible*
$M + A \rightarrow D$ *slow*

Mechanism 2: $B \rightleftharpoons M$ *fast-forward reversible*
$M + A \rightarrow C + X$ *slow*
$A + X \rightarrow D$ *fast*

Mechanism 3: $A + B \rightleftharpoons M$ *fast-forward reversible*
$M + A \rightarrow C + X$ *slow*
$X \rightarrow D$ *fast*

13. The reaction of NO and O_2 gases likely occurs according to the following mechanism.
Step 1: $NO(g) + O_2(g) \rightleftharpoons NO_3(g)$ *fast-forward reversible*
Step 2: $NO_3(g) + NO(g) \rightarrow 2\,NO_2(g)$ *slow*

(a) Show how the two steps combine to give the overall reaction.

(b) Determine the rate law for the overall reaction.

14. You propose the following three-step mechanism for a reaction. The second step is rate determining.

$NH_3(aq) + OBr^-(aq) \rightleftharpoons NH_2Br(aq) + OH^-(aq)$

$NH_2Br(aq) + NH_3(aq) \rightarrow N_2H_5^+(aq) + Br^-(aq)$

$N_2H_5^+(aq) + OH^-(aq) \rightarrow N_2H_4(aq) + H_2O(l)$

(a) Show how the three steps combine to give the overall reaction.

(b) Identify any catalysts and/or intermediates.

(c) Determine the rate law predicted by this mechanism.

1.7 Activity: A Molecular View Of a Reaction Mechanism

Question

How can you determine the mechanism for a reaction given a "molecular view"?

Background

Two series of "snapshots" of a reacting system taken several microseconds apart are available for viewing. The first set is of an uncatalyzed reaction. The second set is of the same reaction, but it is catalyzed.

Uncatalyzed reaction: Reactants are B + G; Product is BG.

Snapshot 1

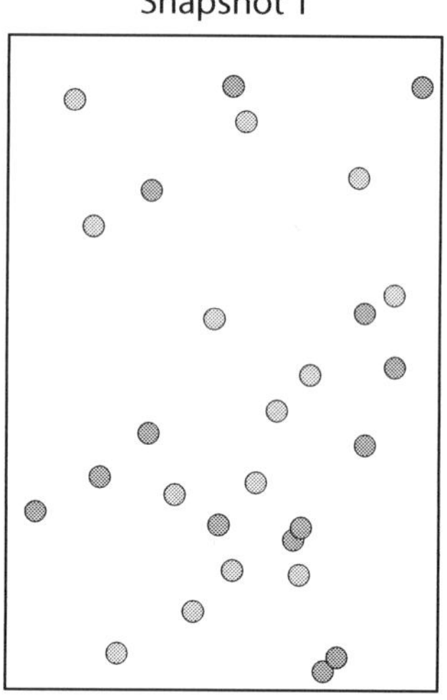

Snapshot 2

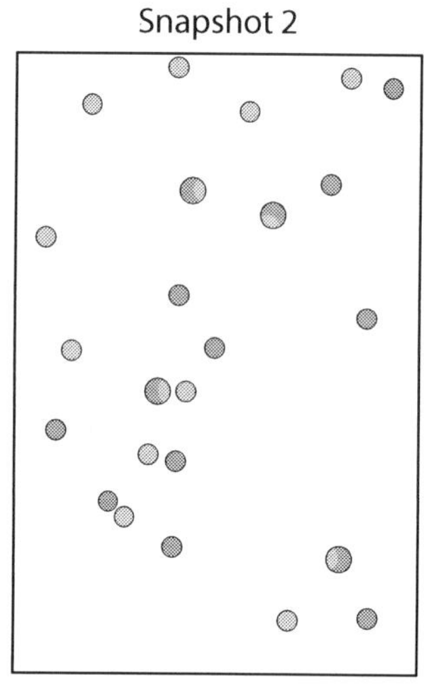

Snapshot 3

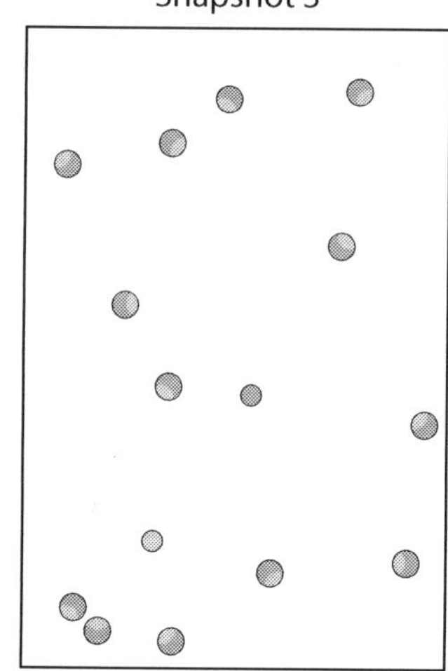

Catalyzed reaction: Reactants are the same as above. Catalyst R added.

Snapshot 1

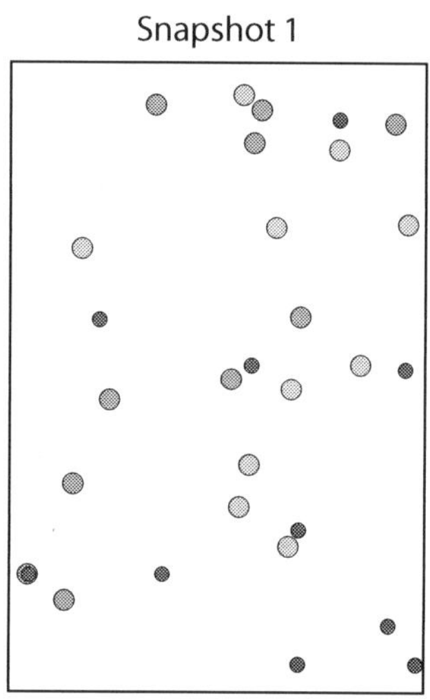

Snapshot 2

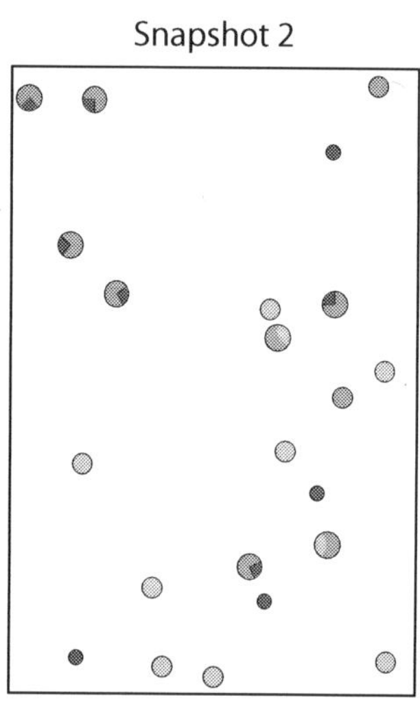

Snapshot 3

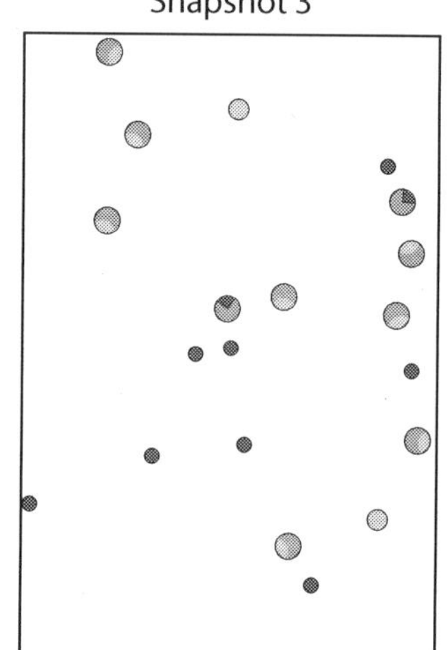

Procedure

1. Determine an equation that represents the uncatalyzed reaction.

2. Determine the reactions that represent the two-step mechanism for the catalyzed reaction.

   Step 1:

   Step 2:

   Overall Reaction:

Results and Discussion

1. Show how steps 1 and 2 sum to give the overall catalyzed reaction.

2. How does the overall reaction compare with the uncatalyzed reaction?

3. Identify the catalyst in the mechanism.

4. Identify any and all intermediates in the mechanism.

5. How would the time passed from snapshots 1 through 3 in the catalyzed series compare with the time for the uncatalyzed series?

6. Assume the second step in the catalyzed series is rate-determining. How would the time passed between snapshots 1 and 2 compare to the time passed between snapshots 2 and 3?

7. For the catalyzed reaction, how would the addition of more B affect the overall reaction rate? More G? Explain your answers.

2 Chemical Equilibrium

This chapter focuses on the following AP Big Idea from the College Board:

- Big Idea 6: Any bond or intermolecular attraction that can be formed can be broken. These two processes are in a dynamic competition, sensitive to initial conditions and external perturbations.

By the end of this chapter, you should be able to do the following:

- Explain the concept of chemical equilibrium with reference to reacting systems
- Predict, with reference to entropy and enthalpy, whether reacting systems will reach equilibrium
- Apply Le Châtelier's principle to the shifting of equilibrium
- Apply the concept of equilibrium to a commercial or industrial process
- Draw conclusions from the equilibrium constant expression
- Perform calculations to evaluate the changes in the value of K_{eq} and in concentrations of substances within an equilibrium system

By the end of this chapter, you should know the meaning of these **key terms**:

- chemical equilibrium
- closed system
- dynamic equilibrium
- enthalpy
- entropy
- equilibrium concentration
- equilibrium constant expression
- equilibrium shift
- Haber process
- heterogeneous reaction
- homogeneous reaction
- ICE table
- K_{eq}
- Le Châtelier's principle
- macroscopic properties
- open system
- PE diagram

When the number of shoppers travelling between the two floors on the escalators is equal, the crowd has reached equilibrium.

Edvantage Science AP Chemistry 2

Chapter 2

Traffic Light Study Guide

Section	Page	I can …	Red	Yellow	Green
2.1	98 - 99	Define *chemical equilibrium* and determine equivalent reaction rates at equilibrium.	○	○	○
	99 - 100	State the criteria for a system to be at chemical equilibrium.	○	○	○
	101	Describe how chemical equilibria are achieved.	○	○	○
2.2	108	State *Le Chatelier's principle*.	○	○	○
	108 - 109	Use Le Chatelier's principle to describe how an equilibrium system will respond to adding or removing, some reactant or product.	○	○	○
	111 – 113	Explain in terms of forward and reverse reaction rates how an equilibrium will respond to adding or removing, reactant or product.	○	○	○
	114	Describe and explain how changing the surface area of a heterogeneous reaction or adding a catalyst affects an equilibrium.	○	○	○
	114	Define *equilibrium position*.	○	○	○
2.3	120 - 128	Use Le Chatelier's principle to describe how an equilibrium system will respond to changing its volume.	○	○	○
	123 – 124	Explain in terms of forward and reverse reaction rates how an equilibrium system will respond to changing its volume.	○	○	○
	125 – 128	Use Le Chatelier's principle to describe how an equilibrium system will respond to changing its temperature.	○	○	○
	127 - 128	Explain in terms of forward and reverse reaction rates how an equilibrium shifts in response to changing temperature.	○	○	○
	129 - 130	Describe the Haber-Bosch Process and discuss how chemists regulate its reacting conditions to optimize its production rate.	○	○	○
2.4	138	Define *entropy*.	○	○	○
	138 – 139	Describe some factors that influence a particle's or compound's entropy.	○	○	○
	139 – 140	Predict whether entropy increases or decreases during certain reactions by using factors that commonly govern entropy change.	○	○	○
	142	Cite the two thermodynamic "drives" that determine an equilibrium's position (far left, somewhat centered, far right)	○	○	○
	142 – 144	Predict an equilibrium's position from its thermodynamics and vice-versa.	○	○	○
	145	Define a *spontaneous* process and relate that to chemical equilibrium	○	○	○

Edvantage Science AP Chemistry 2

Chapter 2

Traffic Light Study Guide

Section	Page	I can ...	Red	Yellow	Green
2.5	149	State the *equilibrium law* and determine a reaction's equilibrium constant (K_{eq}) from its equilibrium concentrations.	○	○	○
	150 – 152	Relate a reaction's equilibrium constant to its equilibrium position.	○	○	○
	152	State the only change of conditions that will change a chemical equation's equilibrium constant.	○	○	○
	153	Determine the equilibrium expression for a chemical equation.	○	○	○
	154	Determine the equilibrium constant for a chemical equation given the equilibrium constant for the reverse equation or the same equation with different coefficients.	○	○	○
	155	Determine the direction a system will proceed to achieve equilibrium, given its reactant and product concentrations and its K_{eq}.	○	○	○
	156 - 157	Recognize equilibria that do not strictly abide by Le Chatelier's principle.	○	○	○
2.6	163 – 164	Calculate a reaction's equilibrium constant, given the initial concentrations of the reactants and any one reactant's or product's equilibrium concentration.	○	○	○
	165 – 167	Calculate a reaction's equilibrium concentrations, given its equilibrium constant and the initial concentrations of its reactants.	○	○	○
	169	Calculate a reaction's initial concentrations, given its equilibrium constant and any one reactant's or product's equilibrium concentration.	○	○	○
	171 - 172	Calculate K_p for a gaseous equilibrium, given the partial pressures of its reactants and products at equilibrium or given its K_c.	○	○	○

For more support in AP Chemistry 2, go to edvantagescience.com

2.1 Introduction to Dynamic Equilibrium

1. Identify each of the following as being either an *equilibrium* or a *steady state*:
   (a) As bees go back and forth from their hive to a flowerbed, the number of bees inside the hive and at the flowerbed remains constant.

   (b) Despite people checking in and out of a motel each day, the number of guests registered at the motel each night remains constant.

   (c) During a basketball game, team members are frequently being substituted in and out of the game. There are always five players on the floor and seven players on the bench.

   (d) Two new students enroll in your chemistry class each day because they hear from their friends how interesting the class is. Unfortunately two students also withdraw each day.

   (e) Shoppers at the Hotel California Mall can never leave (but it's a lovely place). Shoppers travel back and forth on escalators between the mall's two levels though the number of shoppers on each level never changes.

2. An equilibrium exists when a reaction's forward rate equals its reverse rate. Answer the questions below for the following equilibrium:

$$2\,NO(g) + Cl_2(g) \rightleftharpoons 2\,NOCl(g)$$

   (a) Do the moles of NO consumed per second equal the moles of NO produced per second?

   (b) Do the moles of NO consumed per second equal the moles of NOCl consumed per second?

   (c) Do the moles of NOCl produced per second equal the moles of Cl_2 consumed per second?

   (d) Do the grams of NO consumed per second equal the grams of NO produced per second?

   (e) Do the grams of NO consumed per second equal the grams of NOCl consumed per second?

3. $H_2(g)$ is being consumed at a rate of 0.012 mol/s in the following equilibrium:

$$N_2(g) + 3\,H_2(g) \rightleftharpoons 2\,NH_3(g)$$

(a) How many moles of N_2 are being produced and consumed each second?

(b) How many grams of NH_3 are being produced and consumed each second?

4. Melting and evaporating are physical changes, not chemical changes, but changes of physical state can also form dynamic equilibria.

(a) An ice cube floats in a water bath held at 0°C. The size of the ice cube remains constant because the ice is melting at the same rate as the water is freezing. Describe and explain what you would observe if the temperature of the water bath was increased slightly.

(b) The water level in a flask drops as water evaporates from it. The flask is then closed using a rubber stopper. The water level continues to drop for a while but eventually holds steady. Explain why the water level is no longer falling. (Has the evaporation stopped?)

5. A chemist observes a closed system at a constant temperature in which no macroscopic changes are occurring. To determine whether or not the system is at equilibrium, the chemist increases its temperature and notes a change in the properties of the system. Can you be sure that this system is at equilibrium? Explain your answer.

6. Nobel laureate (prize winner) Ilya Prigogine coined the term *dissipative structures* for systems such as candle flames that are in steady state. The chemical reaction for burning one type of wax is:

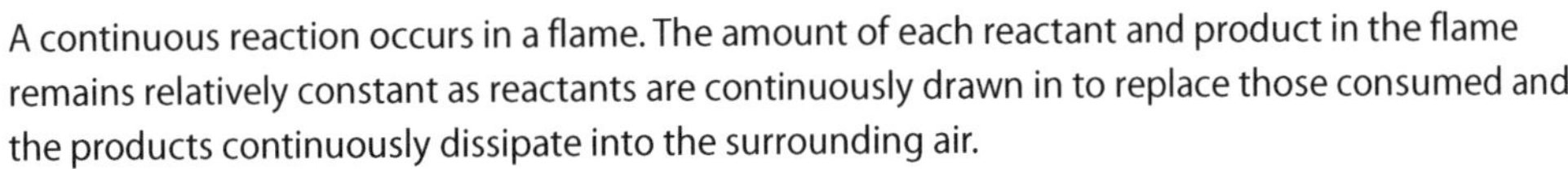

$$C_{25}H_{52}(g) + 38\,O_2(g) \rightarrow 25\,CO_2(g) + 26\,H_2O(g)$$

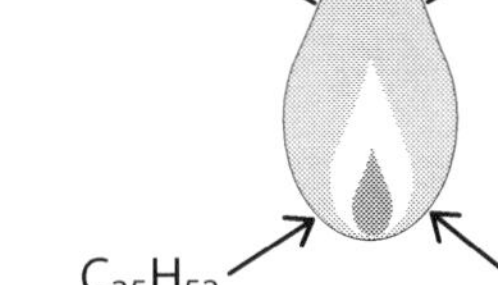

A continuous reaction occurs in a flame. The amount of each reactant and product in the flame remains relatively constant as reactants are continuously drawn in to replace those consumed and the products continuously dissipate into the surrounding air.

(a) How is this situation like an equilibrium?

(b) How is this situation different from an equilibrium?

Fascinate your friends by blowing out a candle flame and then re-igniting the evaporating paraffin gas by placing a lit match a couple centimeters above the wick. Try it!

7. Clock reactions are often used to demonstrate the effect of concentration and temperature on reaction rates. The distinctive aspect of clock reactions is a long delay followed by a sudden appearance of product. This peculiar behavior frequently results from a cyclic mechanism. Consider the mechanism of the iodine clock reaction below:

Step 1 $3\,HSO_3^- + IO_3^- \rightarrow I^- + 3\,H^+ + 3\,SO_4^{2-}$
Step 2 $10\,I^- + 12\,H^+ + 2\,IO_3^- \rightarrow 6\,I_2 + 6\,H_2O$
Step 3 $I_2 + H_2O + HSO_3^- \rightarrow 2\,I^- + 3\,H^+ + SO_4^{2-}$

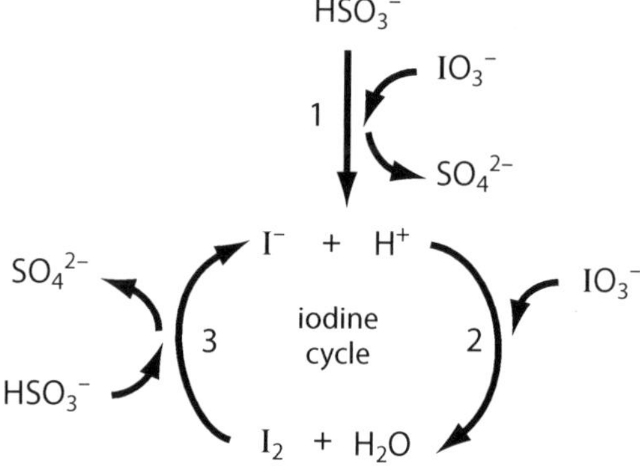

Why is the two-step iodine cycle at the end of this mechanism not at equilibrium even when the two steps are proceeding at the same rate?

8. When considering equilibria, chemists sometimes forget that the forward and reverse reactions may occur through a series of steps. Consider the following reaction mechanism approaching equilibrium:

Step 1:	$2\,NO + H_2 \rightarrow N_2 + H_2O_2$
Step 2:	$H_2O_2 + H_2 \rightarrow 2\,H_2O$
Overall:	$2\,NO + 2\,H_2 \rightarrow N_2 + 2\,H_2O$

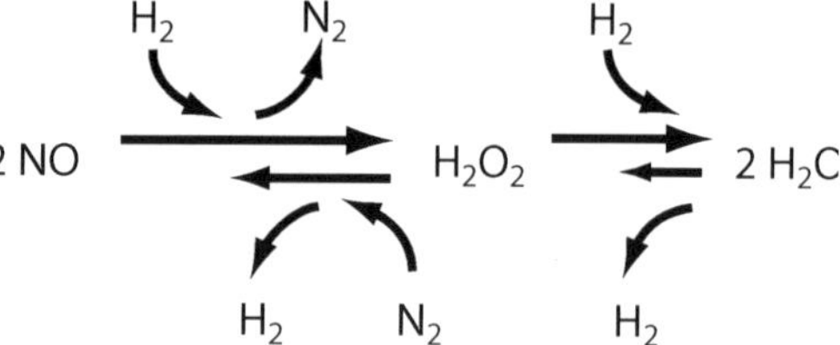

If a reaction is at equilibrium, every step in its mechanism must be at equilibrium. When the above reaction establishes equilibrium, how do you know that:

(a) step 1 must be at equilibrium?

(b) step 2 must be at equilibrium?

9. A chemical reaction achieves equilibrium 20 s after it is initiated. Plot and label the forward reaction rate and the reverse reaction rate as a function of time from $t = 0$ s (initiation) until $t = 30$ s. (Caution: This is **not** the same kind of plot as in Figure 2.1.3. Here you are plotting the rate as a function of time whereas in Figure 2.1.3, we plotted the concentration of reactants and products as a function of time.)

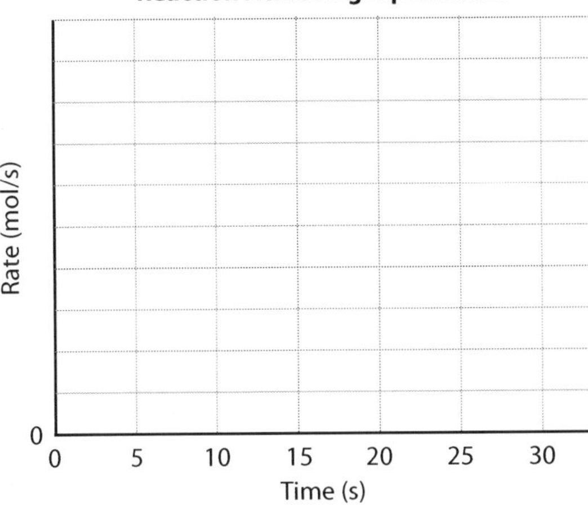

10. Nitrogen dioxide gas is placed in a sealed flask.

$$2\ NO_2(g) \rightarrow N_2O_4(g)$$

orange colorless

(a) What would you see as the reaction approaches equilibrium?

(b) Describe the change in the concentrations of reactants and products as the reaction approaches equilibrium.

(c) Describe the change in the forward and reverse rates as the reaction approaches equilibrium.

11. A system at equilibrium has all of its reactants suddenly removed. Describe how the system would restore equilibrium in terms of its forward and reverse reaction rates and its reactant and product concentrations.

2.1 Activity: A Mathematical Model of Dynamic Equilibrium That Makes Cents

Question

Can we use a model to demonstrate how an equilibrium develops?

Background

Chemical equilibrium exists when each reactant and product is being consumed at the same rate that it is being produced. Chemical species are represented by pennies in this model with heads representing reactants and tails representing products.

Procedure

1. Perform this activity in groups of 2 to 4 students. Each group requires 32 pennies and one six-sided die.
2. Begin by placing all 32 pennies on your desk with their head side up.
3. Each round represents 1 s of reaction time. Reactants (heads) have a 50.0% (1/2) chance of turning into products (tails) each round. Products (tails) have a 16.7% (1/6) chance of turning into reactants (heads) each round. For each round:
   (a) For each head: Simply flip the coin to see whether it remains a head or changes to a tail. This means that in round 1 you flip all 32 coins.
   (b) For each tail: Roll a die and only turn the coin over if you roll a 6.

   Note: Although the reactant and product species would actually be mixed, it is easier to keep track of your heads and tails if you put them in separate groups after each round.
4. Use the table and graph provided below to record the number of reactant and product species present after each round. Draw the reactant's and product's plots using different colored pencils.

Time (Round) (s)	No. of Reactant Species (Heads)	No. of Product Species (Tails)
0	32	0
1		
2		
3		
4		
5		
6		
7		
8		
9		

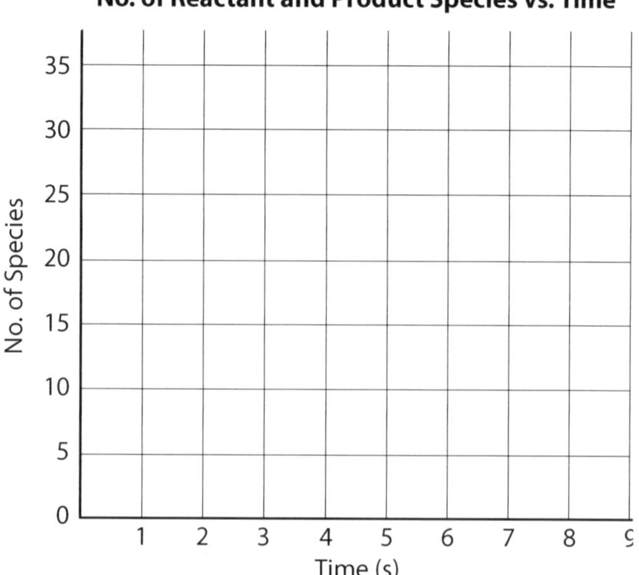

Results and Discussion

1. What does turning over a coin represent in this model?

2. Approximately one-half of the reactants are converted into products each second while only about one-sixth of the products are converted into reactants each second. Identify two possible reasons for the reverse reaction being more difficult to complete than the forward reaction.

3. Why should the percentage of tails that react (turn over) actually increase as the number of tails increases?

2.2 Le Châtelier's Principle

1. Consider the following equilibrium system: $2\,NO(g) + Cl_2(g) \rightleftharpoons 2\,NOCl(g)$

   (a) What does Le Châtelier's principle say will occur if some NO is added to the system?

   (b) In which direction will this system shift in response to the stress?

   (c) Compare the $[Cl_2]$ when equilibrium is reestablished to its concentration before the NO was added.

2. Consider the following equilibrium system: $2\,NO(g) + O_2(g) \rightleftharpoons 2\,NO_2(g)$
   (a) Explain in terms of forward and reverse reaction rates how the system responds to removing some O_2.

   (b) Compare the rates of the forward and reverse reactions when equilibrium is reestablished with the rates before some O_2 was removed.

3. Silver nitrate is added to the equilibrium system:
   $Ag(S_2O_3)_2^{3-}(aq) \rightleftharpoons Ag^+(aq) + 2\,S_2O_3^{2-}(aq)$

   When equilibrium is restored, how will each ion's concentration compare with its concentration before the silver nitrate was added? Explain how you arrived at your answer.

4. Cholesterol is a component of cell membranes and a building block for hormones such as estrogen and testosterone. About 80% of the body's cholesterol is produced by the liver, while the rest comes directly from our diet. There are two forms of cholesterol: a "good" form (HDL) that helps lubricate blood vessels and a "bad" form (LDL) that deposits on the inside of artery walls where it can restrict blood flow. Suppose these two forms could be converted from one to the other via the following "equilibrium" reaction:
   $LDL + X \rightleftharpoons HDL + Y$

   (a) Briefly explain why a drug that removes the bad cholesterol (LDL) would not be completely effective (i.e., it would have a bad side-effect).

   (b) Referring to the above equilibrium, how could a drug company effectively treat people with too high an LDL:HDL ratio?

5. Sulfur dioxide is an important compound in wines, where it acts as an antimicrobial and antioxidant to protect the wine from spoiling. The following equilibrium exists in wines:
$SO_2(aq) + H_2O(l) \rightleftharpoons H^+(aq) + HSO_3^-(aq)$
State whether a winemaker should increase the wine's pH (by removing H^+) or decrease the wine's pH (by adding H^+) to shift the equilibrium toward the active SO_2?

6. Complete the following table using the words "decrease," "same," or "increase" to indicate how the equilibrium concentrations are affected by the stated stress. "Increase" means that when equilibrium is restored, the chemical's concentration is greater than it was before the stress.

$$2\,NH_3(g) \rightleftharpoons N_2(g) + 3\,H_2(g)$$

		Add NH_3	Remove some H_2	Add N_2
Equilibrium Concentration	N_2			
	H_2			
	NH_3			

7. $HP \rightleftharpoons H^+ + P^-$

HP: red; P^-: yellow

The above equilibrium system appears orange due to equal concentrations of HP and P^-.
(a) What action will shift the equilibrium so the solution turns red?

(b) What could be done to shift the equilibrium so the solution turns yellow?

8. Hemoglobin is the protein in red blood cells that transports oxygen to cells throughout your body. Each hemoglobin (Hb) molecule attaches to four oxygen molecules:
$Hb(aq) + 4\,O_2(aq) \rightleftharpoons Hb(O_2)_4(aq)$

In which direction does the above equilibrium shift in each of the following situations:
(a) At high elevations the air pressure is lowered reducing the $[O_2]$ in the blood.

(b) At high altitude, climbers sometimes breathe pressurized oxygen from a tank to increase the $[O_2]$ in the blood.

(c) People who live at higher altitudes produce more hemoglobin.

(d) Carbon monoxide poisoning occurs when carbon monoxide molecules bind to hemoglobin instead of oxygen molecules. Carboxyhemoglobin is even redder than oxyhemoglobin; therefore, one symptom of carbon monoxide poisoning is a flushed face.

9. Explain why neither adding a catalyst nor increasing the surface area of S(*s*) stresses the following equilibrium, even though each of these actions increases the forward reaction rate.
$2\ S(s) + 3\ O_2(g) \rightleftharpoons 2\ SO_3(g)$

10. The following equilibrium exists in an aqueous solution of copper(II) chloride:
$CuCl_4^{2-}(aq) + 4\ H_2O(l) \rightleftharpoons Cu(H_2O)_4^{2+}(aq) + 4\ Cl^-(aq)$
green blue
(a) Some Cl^- is removed by adding some silver nitrate to the solution. The Ag^+ in the silver nitrate precipitates with the Cl^- to produce AgCl(*s*). In what direction will the equilibrium shift?
(b) If the initial equilibrium mixture was blue, what would you observe as a sodium chloride solution was added dropwise to the equilibrium mixture?

11. At t_1 some CO was suddenly removed from the closed system shown below. Equilibrium was reestablished at t_2. Complete the plots to show how the system would respond.
$Ni(s) + 4\ CO(g) \rightleftharpoons Ni(CO)_4(g)$

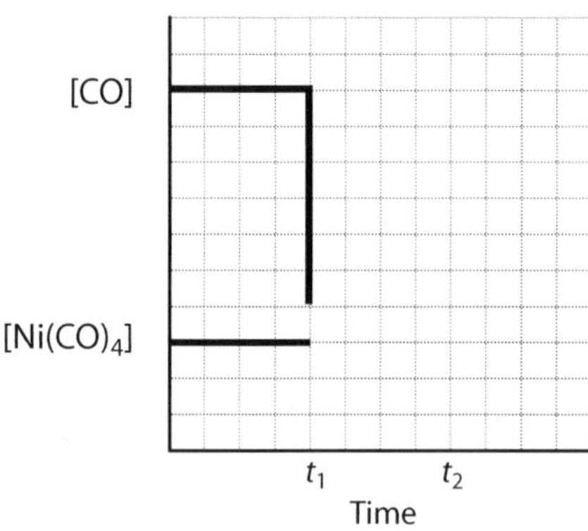

12. Show how the forward and reverse reaction rates respond to having some HOCl suddenly removed from the following system at t_1.
$H_2O(g) + Cl_2O(g) \rightleftharpoons 2\ HOCl(g)$
Use a solid line for the forward rate and a dotted line for the reverse rate. The system re-equilibrates at t_2. The arrow diagram on the right is another way of displaying the same information. You may use it to do your rough work.

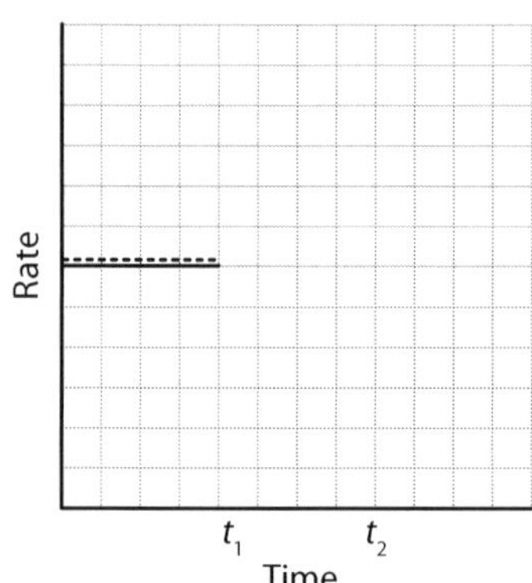

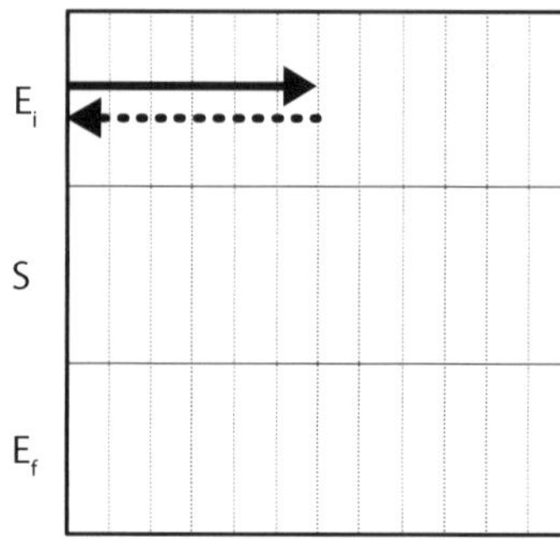

13. Equilibria are often linked through one chemical common to both. Even two equilibria coupled together present an interesting dynamic.

Equilibrium 1

$$Cu^{2+} + 4\,NH_3 \rightleftharpoons Cu(NH_3)_4^{2+}$$

+

$4\,H^+$

Equilibrium 2 ⇅

$4\,NH_4^+$

How would the $[Cu^{2+}]$ be affected by adding some H^+ to this coupled system? Briefly explain using Le Châtelier's principle.

14. Silver acetate has a low solubility in water. A small amount of solid silver acetate is in equilibrium with a saturated solution of its ions.

Equilibrium 1

$$AgCH_3COO(s) \rightleftharpoons Ag^+(aq) + CH_3COO^-(aq)$$

+

$H^+(aq)$

Equilibrium 2 ⇅

$CH_3COOH(aq)$

What would you observe occurring in the beaker as $H^+(aq)$ is added dropwise to the solution? Briefly explain using Le Châtelier's principle.

15. Consider the following equilibrium:

$2\,NO(g) + O_2(g) \rightleftharpoons 2\,NO_2(g)$

Describe how [NO] could be greater than the $[NO_2]$ despite the products being favored at equilibrium.

16. Because few natural systems are closed, many of nature's reversible reactions are perpetually "chasing after" equilibrium. In *At Home in the Universe*, the author, Stuart Kauffman, describes living systems as "persistently displaced from chemical equilibrium." Describe one way to ensure that a reversible reaction never achieves equilibrium.

2.2 Activity: How an Equilibrium System "Copes" With Stress

Question

Can we use our mathematical model to demonstrate how an equilibrium system "copes" with having some reactant added?

Background

Le Châtelier's principle states that any equilibrium system subjected to a stress will restore equilibrium by partially counteracting the stress. Let's test this principle by adding some reactant to the equilibrium we established in the 2.1 Activity.

Procedure

1. Perform this activity in groups of two to four students. Each group requires 48 pennies.
2. Begin by recreating the equilibrium you achieved in the 2.1 Activity by placing 32 pennies on your desk, 8 with their "head" side up and 24 with their "tail" side up.
3. Each round represents 1 s of reaction time. Reactants (heads) have a 50.0% (1/2) chance of turning into products (tails) each round. Products (tails) have a 16.7% (1/6) chance of turning into reactants (heads) each round. For each round:
   (i) For each head: Simply flip the coin to see whether it remains a head or changes to a tail.
   (ii) For each tail: Roll a die and only turn the coin over if you roll a 6.
4. After two rounds, add 16 heads to the reacting mixture and then continue the activity as before until equilibrium has been restored.
5. Use the table and graph provided below to record the number of reactant and product species present after each round.

Time (Round) (s)	No. of Reactant Species (Heads)	No. of Product Species (Tails)
0	8	24
1		
2	+ 16 =	
3		
4		
5		
6		
7		
8		
9		

6. Draw the reactant's plot and the product's plot with different-colored pencils.

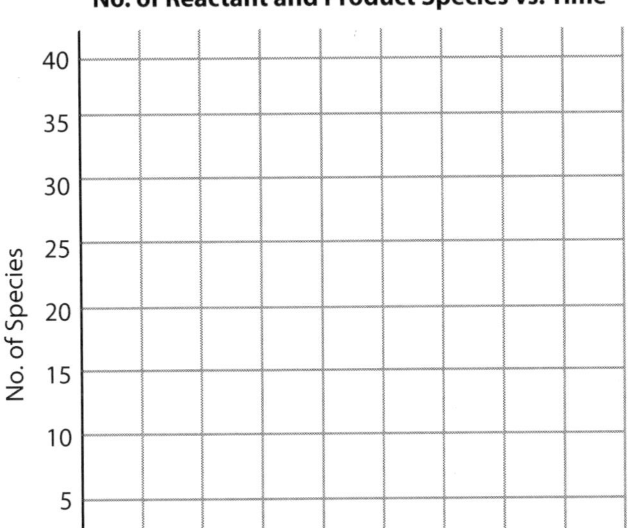

Results and Discussion

1. According to Le Châtelier's principle, the number of heads present when equilibrium is restored could be as few as ________ or as many as ________. Explain.

2. How many heads were present when equilibrium was re-established? ________

2.3 How Equilibria Respond to Volume and Temperature Changes

1. Consider the following equilibrium: $Fe^{3+}(aq) + SCN^{-}(aq) \rightleftharpoons FeSCN^{2+}(aq)$
   (a) In which direction will the system shift if it is diluted? Explain your answer in terms of Le Châtelier's principle.

   (b) Compare the number and the concentration of SCN^{-} ions when equilibrium is restored to their number and concentration before the system was diluted.

2. Explain *in terms of forward and reverse reaction rates* how this system responds to an increase in volume.

$$PCl_5(g) \rightleftharpoons PCl_3(g) + Cl_2(g)$$

3. In which direction does the following equilibrium shift when the gas mixture is compressed? Explain using Le Châtelier's principle *and* in terms of forward and reverse reaction rates.

$$2\ C(s) + O_2(g) \rightleftharpoons 2\ CO(g)$$

4. Describe a situation when equilibrium concentrations change but no stress occurs.

5. Complete the following plots. The system is at equilibrium prior to t_1. At t_1 the volume of the system is suddenly doubled. The system responds to this stress between t_1 and t_2 until it re-equilibrates at t_2.

$$N_2O_4(g) \rightleftharpoons 2\ NO_2(g)$$

6. Show how the forward and reverse reaction rates respond to a sudden increase in the volume of the system at t_1. Use a solid line for the forward rate and a dotted line for the reverse rate. The system restores equilibrium at t_2. The arrow diagram on the right is another way of depicting the same information. You may use it to do your rough work.

$$N_2O_4(g) \rightleftharpoons 2\,NO_2(g)$$

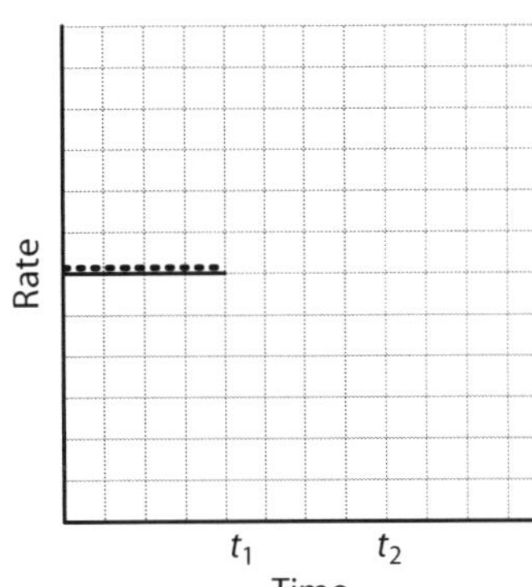

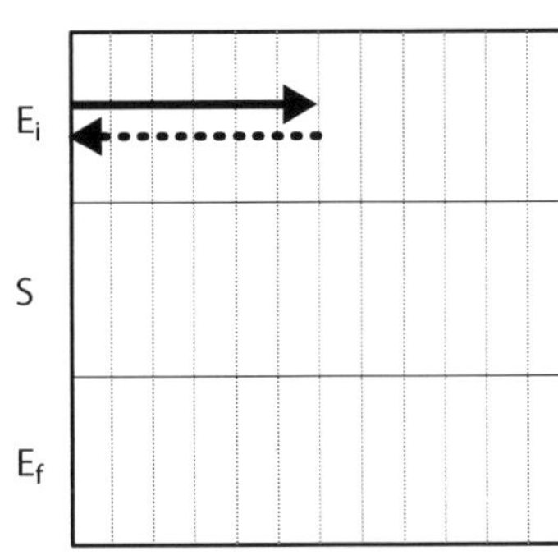

7. The solubility of a substance is its highest possible concentration at a given temperature. Any further solid added to the solution will remain undissolved in equilibrium with the dissolved state. Dissolving sodium sulfate in water is exothermic.

$$Na_2SO_4(s) \rightleftharpoons 2\,Na^+(aq) + SO_4^{2-}(aq) + \text{heat}$$

State whether sodium sulfate will be less soluble or more soluble when the temperature of the solution is increased. Explain.

8. In which direction will the following equilibrium system shift when it is heated?

$$2\,SO_3(g) + 192\text{ kJ/mol} \rightleftharpoons 2\,SO_2(g) + O_2(g)$$

Provide two ways to arrive at this answer.

9. Complete the following plots. The system below is at equilibrium prior to t_1. The system is suddenly cooled at t_1. The system responds to this stress between t_1 and t_2 until it re-equilibrates at t_2.

$$N_2O_4(g) + 57\text{ kJ} \rightleftharpoons 2\,NO_2(g)$$

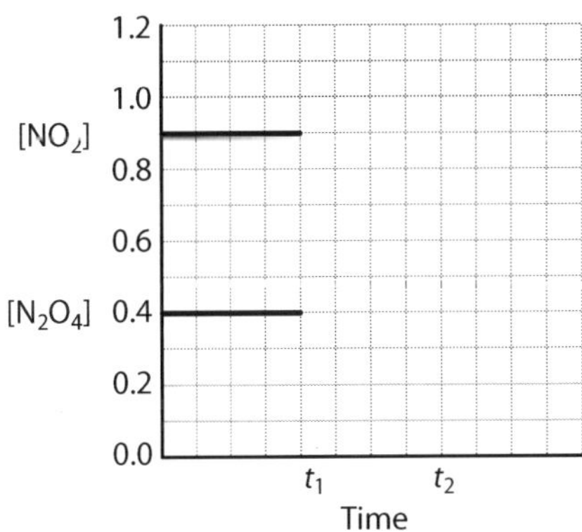

10. Show how the forward and reverse reaction rates respond to a sudden increase in the temperature of the system below at t_1. Use a solid line for the forward rate and a dotted line for the reverse rate. The system restores equilibrium at t_2. The arrow diagram on the right is another way of depicting the same information. You may use it to do your rough work.

$$Ni(s) + 4\,CO(g) \rightleftharpoons Ni(CO)_4(g) \qquad \Delta H = -603 \text{ kJ/mol}$$

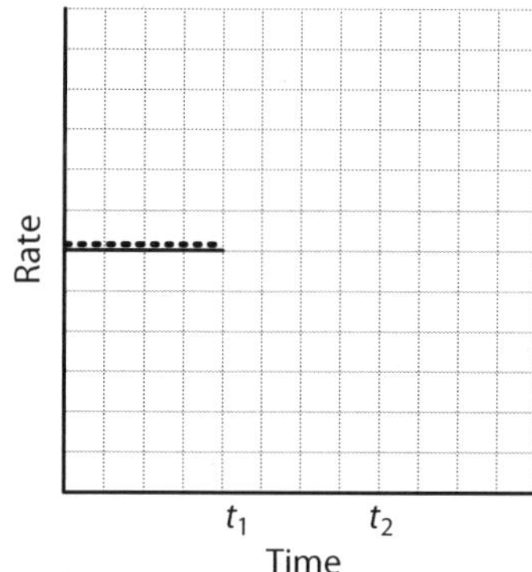

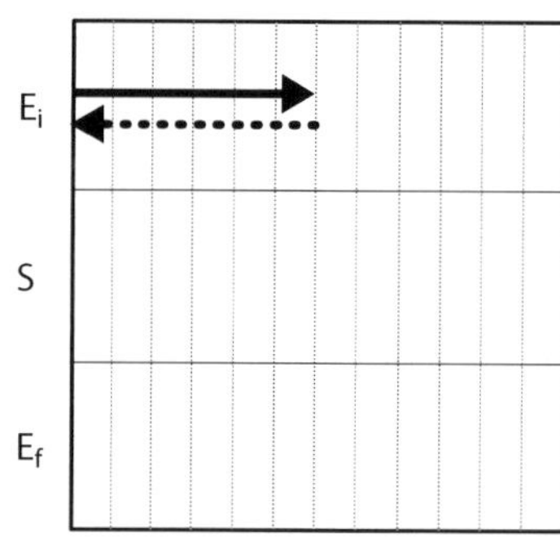

11. $Co(H_2O)_6^{2+}(aq) + 2\,Cl^-(aq) \rightleftharpoons Co(H_2O)_4Cl_2(aq) + 2\,H_2O(l)$
pink — purple

A flask containing the above equilibrium turns from purple to pink when cooled. State whether the forward reaction is endothermic or exothermic. Explain how you arrived at your answer.

12. $A + B \rightleftharpoons AB + 16.8$ kJ/mol

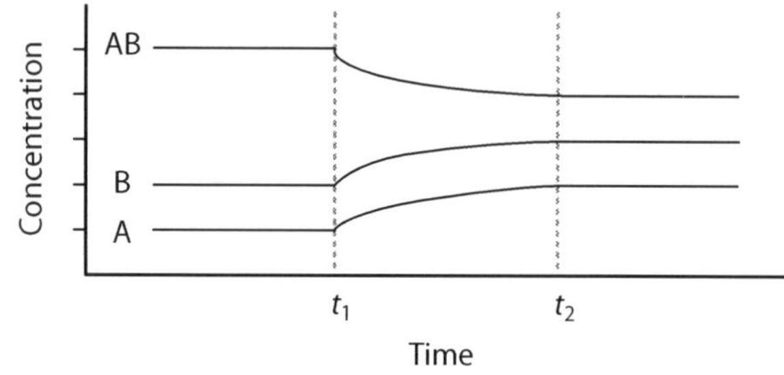

(a) In which direction is the equilibrium system shifting?

(b) What specifically was done to this system at t_1?

13. Explain *in terms of forward and reverse reaction rates* how the equilibrium below responds to a decrease in temperature:

$$N_2(g) + 3\,H_2(g) \rightleftharpoons 2\,NH_3(g) \qquad \Delta H = -92.4 \text{ kJ/mol}$$

14. Why is an equilibrium's endothermic direction more sensitive to temperature changes than its exothermic direction?

15. What conditions of temperature and pressure favor products in the following reaction:

$$PCl_5(g) \rightleftharpoons PCl_3(g) + Cl_2(g) \qquad \Delta H = 238 \text{ kJ/mol}$$

16. Briefly describe the conflicting factors that chemists face when choosing a temperature to perform the Haber-Bosch process.

17. Consider the system below. When equilibrium is restored, how will the number of each type of molecule and the concentration of each substance compare to those before the stress was introduced? Complete the following table using the words "decrease," "same," or "increase."

$$2\,NH_3(g) \rightleftharpoons N_2(g) + 3\,H_2(g) \qquad \Delta H = 92.4 \text{ kJ/mol}$$

		Decrease Volume	Decrease Temperature
Equilibrium concentration	N_2		
	H_2		
	NH_3		
Equilibrium number	N_2		
	H_2		
	NH_3		

18. The graph below shows how forward and reverse reaction rates change as an exothermic reaction goes from initiation to equilibrium. Plot the forward and reverse reaction rates for the same reaction at a higher temperature.

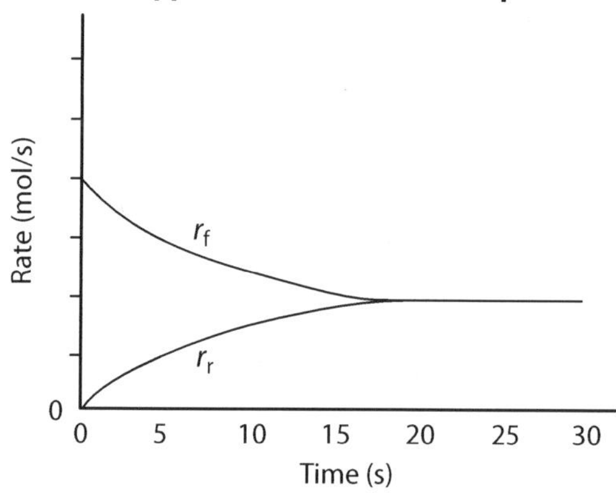

19. Nitric acid is produced commercially by the Ostwald process. The first step of the Ostwald process is:

$$4\,NH_3(g) + 5\,O_2(g) \rightleftharpoons 4\,NO(g) + 6\,H_2O(g) + \text{energy}$$

In which direction will the above system shift in the following situations:

(a) Some NO is added.

(b) Some NH_3 is removed.

(c) The pressure of the system is decreased by increasing the volume.

(d) The temperature of the system is decreased.

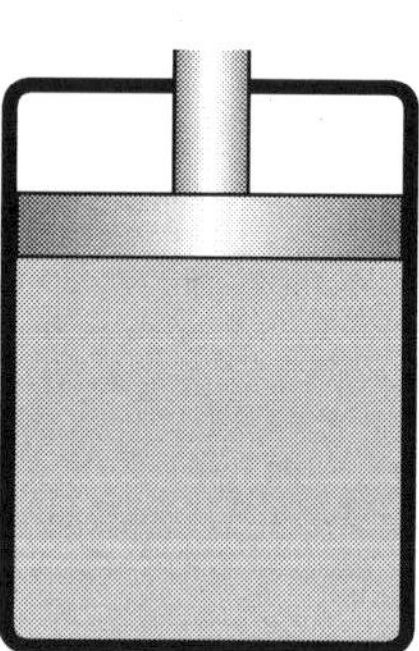

20. A piston supported by gas trapped in a cylinder is a fixed pressure apparatus. As long as the gas in the cylinder is supporting the same piston then its pressure must be constant because it is exerting the same force over the same bottom surface of the piston. If the piston weighs more, then the fixed pressure is greater. Consider the following equilibrium system trapped in a cylinder:

$$PCl_5(g) \rightleftharpoons PCl_3(g) + Cl_2(g)$$

(a) In which direction will the system shift when some weight is added to the piston?

(b) How would this shift affect the apparatus?

21. Complete the following review table.

$N_2(g) + 3\ H_2(g) \rightleftharpoons 2\ NH_3(g) \quad \Delta H = -92.4$ kJ/mol				
Stress	**Le Châtelier Predicts**		**Chemical Kinetics Explains**	
	Response	**Shift**	**Effect**	**Net Rx**
Add H_2	some of the added H_2 removed			
Add NH_3		left		
Remove N_2			r_f decreases	
Decrease volume (compress)				net forward rx
Decrease temperature			r_r decreases more than r_f	

22. Holding the temperature and pressure constant when a reactant or product is added to an equilibrium system is easier said than done. Some SO_3 is added to the following system. Its temperature and pressure are *not* fixed.

$$2\ SO_2(g) + O_2(g) \rightleftharpoons 2\ SO_3(g) + 198\ \text{kJ/mol}$$

(a) In which direction will the system shift in response to the added SO_3?

(b) In which direction will the system shift in response to the small change in pressure resulting from the added SO_3?

(c) In which direction will the system shift in response to the small change in temperature resulting from the increased pressure?

(d) In which direction will the system shift in response to the change in temperature resulting from the system's shift to the added SO_3?

2.3 Activity: Dealing With Pressure

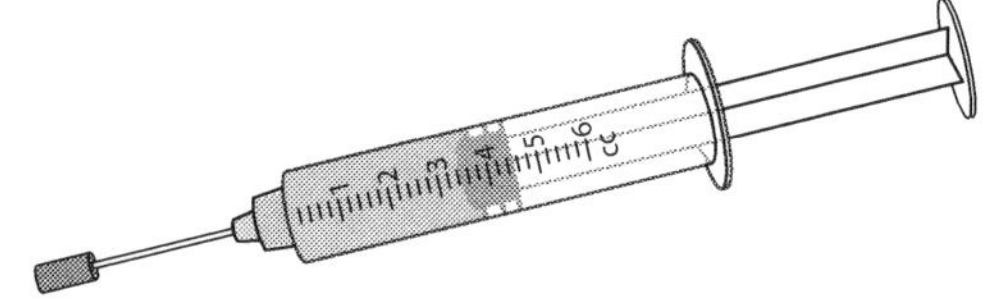

Question

What will a gaseous equilibrium mixture look like at the molecular level as it responds to being compressed?

Background

An equilibrium mixture of colorless dinitrogen tetroxide, $N_2O_4(g)$, and orange nitrogen dioxide, $NO_2(g)$, forms when nitric acid is poured over copper. When this equilibrium mixture is compressed in a plugged syringe, the mixture becomes darker orange as a result of concentrating the NO_2 molecules. Within seconds the mixture's color changes slightly, yet unmistakeably, as the equilibrium shifts in response to the stress.

$$\underset{\text{colorless}}{N_2O_4(g)} + \text{energy} \rightleftharpoons \underset{\text{orange}}{2\ NO_2(g)}$$

Procedure

1. The three diagrams below represent the tube in a syringe. Complete the third diagram by drawing in a possible number of NO_2 and N_2O_4 molecules after the system has responded to the stress and restored equilibrium.
2. Color in the circles underneath each syringe to indicate how pale or dark orange the gas would appear.

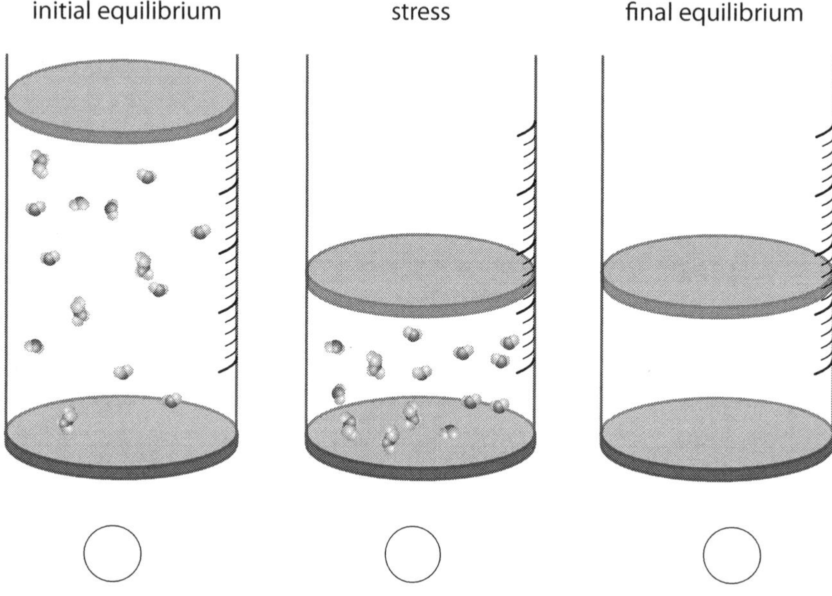

Results and Discussion

1. In response to the compression, the number of NO_2 molecules ______________ and the number of N_2O_4 molecules ______________.

2. Describe the molecules' behavior when the reaction in the syringe is at equilibrium.

3. How would the color of the equilibrium mixture change when the syringe is plunged into an ice bath? Explain.

2.4 Entropy Change versus Enthalpy Change

1. Which substance in each of the following pairs would likely have the greater entropy? Explain.
   (a) $Br_2(l)$ or $Br_2(g)$

   (b) $SO_3(g)$ or $SO_2(g)$

   (c) $Sn(s)$ or $Pb(s)$

2. For each of the following state whether entropy is increasing or decreasing and briefly state your reasoning.
   (a) $2\ NH_3(g) \rightarrow N_2(g) + 3\ H_2(g)$

   (b) $NOCl_2(g) + NO(g) \rightarrow 2\ NOCl(g)$

   (c) $4\ Fe(s) + 3\ O_2(g) \rightarrow 2\ Fe_2O_3(s)$

   (d) $H_2(g) + Cl_2(g) \rightarrow 2\ HCl(g)$

   (e) $WO_3(s) + 3\ H_2(g) \rightarrow W(s) + 3\ H_2O(g)$

3. State whether each of the following reactions will achieve *equilibrium* with a reasonable amount of reactants and products, go almost to *completion*, or virtually *not occur*.
   (a) $4\ NH_3(g) + 5\ O_2(g) \rightarrow 4\ NO(g) + 6\ H_2O(g)$ $\quad \Delta H = -907.2$ kJ/mol

   (b) $N_2(g) + 2\ O_2(g) \rightarrow 2\ NO_2(g)$ $\quad \Delta H = +68$ kJ/mol

   (c) $PCl_3(g) + Cl_2(g) \rightarrow PCl_5(g)$ $\quad \Delta H = -92.5$ kJ/mol

   (d) $S(s) + O_2(g) \rightarrow SO_2(g)$ $\quad \Delta H = -297$ kJ/mol

4. For the following reaction, state whether the forward reaction is endothermic or exothermic, given that the two thermodynamic drives are opposed to each other. Explain your reasoning.
   $CaCO_3(s) \rightleftharpoons CaO(s) + CO_2(g)$

5. Describe the thermodynamics of a reaction that establishes equilibrium so far toward reactants that it is said to virtually not occur.

6. The following equilibrium has a reasonable proportion of reactants and products. State whether entropy is increasing or decreasing during the forward reaction. Explain your reasoning.

$CO_2(g) + NO(g) \rightleftharpoons NO_2(g) + CO(g) \quad \Delta H = +82$ kJ/mol

7. Given that equilibrium is established with a reasonable proportion of reactants and products, in what direction will the system shift when the temperature is decreased? Explain your reasoning.

$2\ SO_2(g) + O_2(g) \rightleftharpoons 2\ SO_3(g)$

8. Why does a reaction that has both thermodynamic drives toward products (the drive toward increasing entropy and the drive toward decreasing enthalpy) not go entirely to completion?

2.4 Activity: Imitating Disorder

Question

Can you place some black dots in a matrix so that they appear to your classmates to be randomly distributed?

Background

When people attempt to randomize objects in space or time, they tend to err toward an even distribution. Let's see if you and your classmates can identify which of each other's two matrices contains the set of dots that are actually randomly distributed.

Procedure

1. Attempt to randomly distribute 12 dots within the squares of one of the two matrices below. You may place more than one dot within a square.
2. Randomly place a single dot *in the other matrix* by rolling a pair of dice twice to determine the row and column to place the dot in (e.g., a 1-1 roll would place the dot in the upper left hand corner of the matrix). Repeat this technique 11 more times to produce a matrix that actually contains 12 randomly distributed dots.

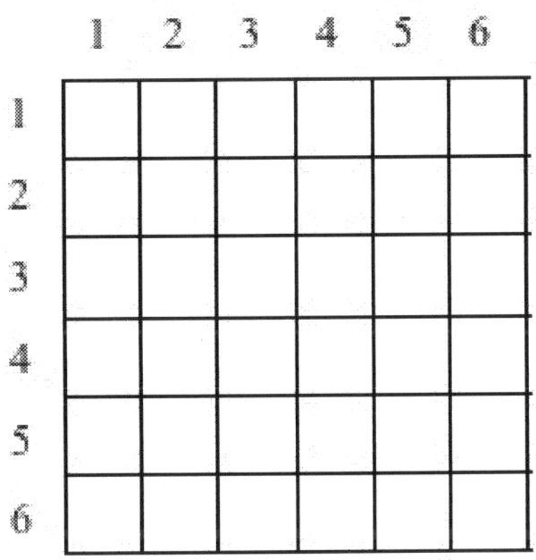

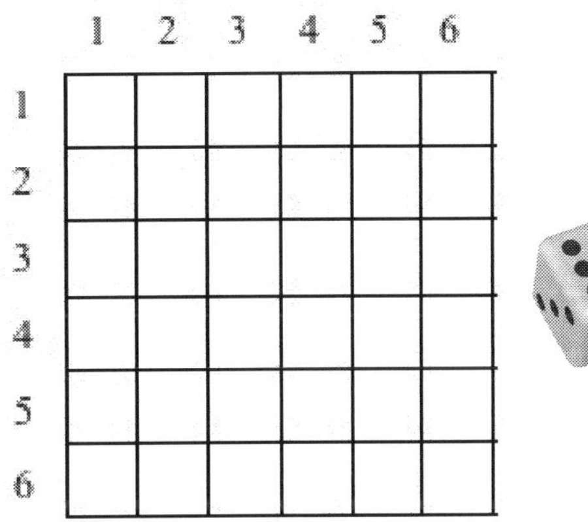

3. Exchange books with 10 classmates. Each time, attempt to identify which of your classmate's two matrices contains the set of dots that are actually randomly distributed.

Results and Discussion

1. Keep a record (卌) in the table below of how many of your classmates chose correctly and how many times you chose correctly.

Your Guesses	
Correct	Incorrect

Your Classmates' Guesses	
Correct	Incorrect

If a person can't tell the difference between the two matrices then there is still a 50% chance that the person will choose the correct matrix. There is only a 17% probability that 7 or more of the 10 people could pick the correct (random) matrix by chance. If this happens, we'll declare your fake "busted." Likewise, if you can correctly identify the random distribution 7 out of 10 times then we'll declare you "randomly gifted."

Each trial tests two things: a person's ability to fake a random distribution and another person's ability to spot the fake. Correctly spotting the random distribution could indicate a "poor" fake or a "good" spotter.

2. Look around the room at your classmates' results and comment on whether there is a relationship between people who are good at faking random patterns and people who are good at recognizing random patterns.

2.5 The Equilibrium Constant

1. At a given temperature the forward and reverse rate equations for the following reaction are as shown (the units for the rate constants are left out for simplicity):

   $2\ N_2O_5(g) \rightleftharpoons 2\ N_2O_4(g) + O_2(g)$

   $r_f = 2.7 \times 10^{-3}\ [N_2O_5]^2$ $\qquad$ $r_r = 4.3 \times 10^{-2}\ [N_2O_4]^2[O_2]$

   Derive the equilibrium constant, K_{eq}, for this reaction at this temperature.

2. A student claims that the coefficients in balanced chemical equations provide the ratio of the chemicals present at equilibrium? For example, consider the following equation.

   $2\ NO(g) + Cl_2(g) \rightleftharpoons 2\ NOCl(g)$

   The student asserts that the equation tells us that the ratio of the equilibrium concentrations will be 2 NO: 1 Cl_2: 2 NOCl. Is the student correct? If not, what do the coefficients represent?

3. Write the equilibrium expression for each of the following:

   (a) $HNO_2\ (aq) \rightleftharpoons H^+(aq) + NO_2^-(aq)$

   (b) $2\ SO_3(g) \rightleftharpoons 2\ SO_2(g) + O_2(g)$

   (c) $4\ NH_3(g) + 5\ O_2(g) \rightleftharpoons 4\ NO(g) + 6\ H_2O(g)$

4. A 2.0 L flask contains 0.38 mol $CH_4(g)$, 0.59 mol $C_2H_2(g)$, and 1.4 mol $H_2(g)$ at equilibrium. Calculate the equilibrium constant, K_{eq}, for the reaction:

   $2\ CH_4(g) \rightleftharpoons C_2H_2(g) + 3\ H_2(g)$

5. A cylinder contains 0.12 M $COBr_2$, 0.060 M CO, and 0.080 M Br_2 at equilibrium. The volume of the cylinder is suddenly doubled.
$COBr_2(g) \rightleftharpoons CO(g) + Br_2(g)$
(a) What is the molar concentration of each gas immediately after the volume of the cylinder is doubled?

(b) Explain, in terms of Le Châtelier's principle, why the system shifts right to restore equilibrium.

(c) The system re-equilibrates by converting 0.010 M $COBr_2$ into CO and Br_2. Verify that the original equilibrium concentrations and the re-established equilibrium concentrations provide the same value when substituted into the reaction's equilibrium expression.

6. A closed flask contains 0.65 mol/L N_2 and 0.85 mol/L H_2 at equilibrium. What is the $[NH_3]$?
$N_2(g) + 3\,H_2(g) \rightleftharpoons 2\,NH_3(g)$ $\quad K_{eq} = 0.017$

7. A 1.0 L flask is injected simultaneously with 4.0 mol N_2, 3.0 mol H_2, and 8.0 mol NH_3. In what direction will the reaction proceed to achieve equilibrium? Show your mathematical reasoning.
$N_2(g) + 3\,H_2(g) \rightleftharpoons 2\,NH_3(g)$ $\quad K_{eq} = 1.0$

8. Write the equilibrium expression for each of the following:
(a) $Fe(s) + 2\,H^+(aq) \rightleftharpoons H_2(g) + Fe^{2+}(aq)$

(b) $2\,I^-(aq) + Cl_2(aq) \rightleftharpoons I_2(s) + 2\,Cl^-(aq)$

(c) $CaO(s) + CO_2(g) \rightleftharpoons CaCO_3(s)$

(d) $CO_2(g) \rightleftharpoons CO_2(aq)$ (Include each chemical's phase in the equilibrium expression.)

(e) $2\ Na_2O(s) \rightleftharpoons 4\ Na(l) + O_2(g)$

9. Write the chemical equation and the equilibrium expression for the equilibrium that develops when:
   (a) Gaseous chlorine dissolves in water.

   (b) Gaseous carbon tetrachloride decomposes into solid carbon and chlorine gas.

   (c) Solid magnesium oxide reacts with sulfur dioxide gas and oxygen gas to produce solid magnesium sulfate.

10. $2\ NOCl(g) \rightleftharpoons 2\ NO(g) + Cl_2(g)$ $K_{eq} = 8.0 \times 10^{-2}$ at 462°C
    For each of the following, what is the K_{eq} at 462°C?
    (a) $NOCl(g) \rightleftharpoons NO(g) + \frac{1}{2}\ Cl_2(g)$

    (b) $2\ NO(g) + Cl_2(g) \rightleftharpoons 2\ NOCl(g)$

    (c) $NO(g) + \frac{1}{2}\ Cl_2(g) \rightleftharpoons NOCl(g)$

11. How would each of the following stresses affect the equilibrium constant, K_{eq}, for:

$2\,CO(g) + O_2(g) \rightleftharpoons 2\,CO_2(g) \qquad \Delta H = -31$ kJ/mol

(a) Add some $CO_2(g)$?

(b) Decrease the volume of the reaction vessel (at a constant temperature)?

(c) Increase the temperature?

(d) Add a catalyst?

12. Can you infer that reactants are favored in the reaction below because $K_{eq} < 1$? Explain.

$C(s) + H_2O(g) \rightleftharpoons CO(g) + H_2(g) \qquad K_{eq} = 0.16$

13. Consider the following two equilibria:

(a) $2\,SO_3(g) \rightleftharpoons 2\,SO_2(g) + O_2(g) \qquad K_{eq} = 0.25$

(b) $PCl_5(g) \rightleftharpoons PCl_3(g) + Cl_2(g) \qquad K_{eq} = 0.50$

Given that their initial reactant concentrations are equal, can you infer from their equilibrium constants that the first equilibrium has a lower percent yield than the second equilibrium? Explain.

14. Consider the following equilibrium:

$2\,KClO_3(s) \rightleftharpoons 2\,KCl(s) + 3\,O_2(g) \qquad \Delta H = 56$ kJ/mol

Compare the $[O_2]$ when equilibrium is re-established to its concentration before:

(a) some $KClO_3(s)$ is added.

(b) some $O_2(g)$ is removed.

(c) the temperature is decreased.

2.5 Activity: What's My Constant?

Question

How can you determine the mathematical relationship that is common to three sets of numbers? Of course, it's a lot easier to discover the relationship when you know that one actually exists!

Background

Do you think that you could have reasoned or recognized that different sets of equilibrium concentrations have a common mathematical relationship? The Norwegian chemists Cato Maximilian Guldberg and Peter Waage proposed the equilibrium law in 1864 after observing many different sets of equilibrium concentrations.

Procedure

Each set of numbers in the table below satisfies the formula A – B + C = 5.

Set	A	B	C
1	10	6	1
2	3	1	3
3	– 4	2	11

A – B + C = 5 ____________

1. Each set of numbers in the table below can also be substituted into a common formula yielding a constant. Determine that formula.

Set	A	B	C
1	18	3	9
2	6	22	2
3	5	10	15

Easy

____

2. Repeat procedure step 1 for each table below.

Set	A	B	C
1	3	4	20
2	5	37	3
3	14	24	88

Challenging

____

Set	A	B	C
1	7	13	20
2	0	5	9
3	3	10	33

Really Hard

____

Results and Discussion

1. Briefly describe the method(s) you used to determine the expression for each collection of data.

2. How successful were you and your colleagues at this task?

3. Why do you not need anyone to mark this activity to know whether or not you were successful?

2.6 Equilibrium Problems

1. Complete the following ICE tables.

(a)

	$2\,CH_4(g) \rightleftharpoons$	$C_2H_2(g)$ +	$3\,H_2(g)$
I	6.0	0	0
C			
E		1.5	

(b)

	$N_2(g)$ +	$3\,H_2(g) \rightleftharpoons$	$2\,NH_3(g)$
I		5.0	0
C			
E	2.0		1.0

2. During an experiment, 3.0 mol of NO_2 are injected into a 1.0 L flask at 55°C. At equilibrium, the flask contains 1.2 mol of N_2O_4.

$2\,NO_2(g) \rightleftharpoons N_2O_4(g)$

(a) What is the $[NO_2]$ at equilibrium?

(b) What is K_{eq} for this reaction at 55°C?

3. Equal volumes of 3.60 M A^{2+} and 6.80 M B^- are mixed. After the reaction, equilibrium is established with $[B^-] = 0.40$ M.

$A^{2+}(aq) + 3B^-(aq) \rightleftharpoons AB_3^-(aq)$

(a) What is the $[A^{2+}]$ at equilibrium?

(b) Determine K_{eq}.

4. Complete the following ICE tables:

(a)

K_{eq} = 1.20	$H_2(g)$ +	$C_2N_2(g)$ ⇌	2 HCN(g)
I			0
C			
E	5.0	1.5	

(b)

K_{eq} = 1.20	$H_2(g)$ +	$C_2N_2(g)$ ⇌	2 HCN(g)
I	5.4		0
C			
E			3.6

5. The interconversion of the structural isomers glyceraldehyde-3-phospate (G3P) and dihydroxyacetone phosphate (DHAP) is a biochemical equilibrium that occurs during the breakdown of glucose in our cells. What will their concentrations be at equilibrium if the initial concentration of each isomer is 0.020 M?

G3P(*aq*) ⇌ DHAP(*aq*) $K_{eq} = 19$

6. A 1.00 L flask is injected with 0.600 mol of each of the following four gases: H_2, CO_2, H_2O, and CO.

$H_2(g) + CO_2(g) \rightleftharpoons H_2O(g) + CO(g)$ $K_{eq} = 1.69$

(a) What is the $[H_2]$ at equilibrium?

(b) What is the [CO] at equilibrium?

7. A 500 mL flask is injected with 0.72 mol of C_2N_2 and 0.72 mol of H_2. What will the [HCN] be when the system reaches equilibrium?

$H_2(g) + C_2N_2(g) \rightleftharpoons 2\ HCN(g)$ $K_{eq} = 1.20$

8. A 1.0 L flask containing 4.0 mol of H_2 and a 1.0 L flask containing 4.0 mol of F_2 are connected by a valve. The valve is opened to allow the gases to mix in the 2.0 L combined volume.

$H_2(g) + F_2(g) \rightleftharpoons 2\ HF(g)$ $\qquad K_{eq} = 121$

How many moles of H_2 will be present in the system when it equilibrates?

9. A 250 mL flask containing 1.0 g of excess BN(s) is injected with 0.21 mol of $Cl_2(g)$.

$2\ BN(s) + 3\ Cl_2(g) \rightleftharpoons 2\ BCl_3(g) + N_2(g)$ $\qquad K_{eq} = 0.045$

(a) What will the $[BCl_3]$ equal when the system attains equilibrium? (Hint: The math is a bit trickier on this one; you need to take the cube root of each side.)

(b) Would the reaction achieve equilibrium if the flask initially contained 1.0 g of BN(s)? Support your answer with calculations.

10. A flask is injected with 0.60 M C_2H_2 and 0.60 M H_2. Determine the $[H_2]$ at equilibrium by trial and error. Lower the $[C_2H_2]$ and the $[H_2]$ and raise the $[CH_4]$ in appropriate increments until you find a set of concentrations that provides the K_{eq} value when substituted into the equilibrium expression.

$2\ CH_4(g) \rightleftharpoons C_2H_2(g) + 3\ H_2(g)$ $\quad K_{eq} = 2.8$

11. In a 2.00 L flask, 3.00 M H_2, 3.00 M Cl_2, and 7.50 M HCl coexist at equilibrium. A student removes 7.00 mol of HCl from the flask.

(a) What would the concentration of each gas be when equilibrium re-establishes?

	$H_2(g)$ +	$Cl_2(g)$ $\rightleftharpoons$	$2\ HCl(g)$
E_o			
I			
C			
E_f			

(b) Describe how the system's response is consistent with Le Châtelier's principle.

12. A 200.0 mL solution of 0.10 M Fe^{3+}, 0.10 M SCN^-, and 1.8 M $FeSCN^{2+}$ is at equilibrium. The solution is diluted by adding water up to 500.0 mL. Complete the ICE table below and show the algebraic equation that would allow you to solve for the ion concentrations when equilibrium is restored. Do **NOT** solve for *x*.

	$Fe^{3+}(aq)$ +	$SCN^-(aq)$ $\rightleftharpoons$	$FeSCN^{2+}(aq)$
E_o	0.10	0.10	1.8
I			
C			
E_f			

13. In a 500.0 mL flask, 2.5 mol of H_2, 2.5 mol of Br_2, and 5.0 mol of HBr coexist at equilibrium. At 35 s, 2.5 mol of Br_2 is injected into the flask, and the system re-establishes equilibrium at 55 s. Use three different-colored plots on the graph below to show how the concentration of each chemical changes during this period. (This question can be solved algebraically without using the quadratic formula despite not providing a perfect square.)

$H_2(g) + Br_2(g) \rightleftharpoons 2\,HBr(g)$

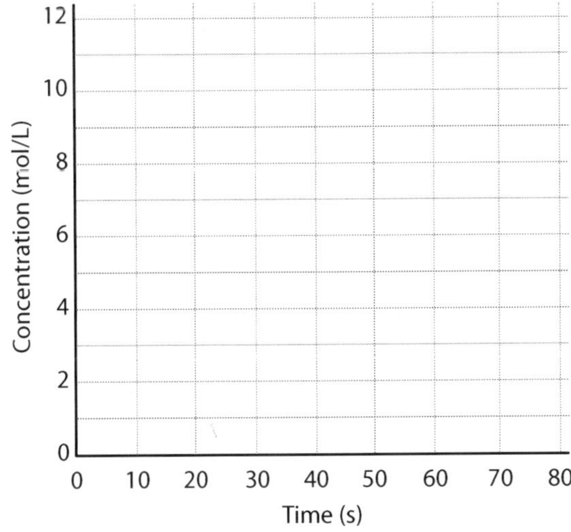

14. Some SO_3 is injected into a 500 mL flask. At equilibrium the $[O_2] = 1.80$ M.

$2\ SO_3(g) \rightleftharpoons 2\ SO_2(g) + O_2(g)$ $\qquad K_{eq} = 3.83 \times 10^{-2}$

(a) What is the $[SO_3]$ at equilibrium?

(b) How many moles of SO_3 were originally injected into the flask?

15. Equal quantities of $H_2(g)$ and $I_2(g)$ are pumped into a flask. At equilibrium the $[HI] = 1.0$ M. What was the initial $[H_2]$?

$H_2(g) + I_2(g) \rightleftharpoons 2\ HI(g)$ $\qquad K_{eq} = 4.0$

16. Some PCl_5 is pumped into a 500 mL flask. The $[PCl_3] = 1.50$ M at equilibrium. What was the initial $[PCl_5]$?

$PCl_5(g) \rightleftharpoons PCl_3(g) + Cl_2(g)$ $\qquad K_{eq} = 2.14$

17. A reaction mixture contains 0.24 mol of NO, 0.10 mol of O_2, and 1.20 mol of NO_2 at equilibrium in a 1.0 L container. How many moles of O_2 would need to be added to the mixture to increase the amount of NO_2 to 1.30 mol when equilibrium is re-established?

$2\ NO(g) + O_2(g) \rightleftharpoons 2\ NO_2(g)$

18. Write the K_p expression for each of the following equations:

(a) $PCl_5(g) \rightleftharpoons PCl_3(g) + Cl_2(g)$

(b) $P_4(s) + 5\ O_2(g) \rightleftharpoons 2\ P_2O_5(g)$

(c) $CO_2(g) + CaO(s) \rightleftharpoons CaCO_3(s)$

19. Calculate K_p for the equilibria in Review Questions 4, 6, and 7 in the previous section.
Review Question 4:

Review Question 6:

Review Question 7:

20. Consider the following reaction:
$2\ SO_2(g) + O_2(g) \rightleftharpoons 2\ SO_3(g)$ $K_p = 0.14$ at 625°C

If a reaction vessel is filled with SO_3 at a partial pressure of 0.10 atm and 0.20 atm each of SO_2 and O_2 gas, is the reaction at equilibrium? If not, in which direction does it proceed to reach equilibrium?

21. The following graph represents partial pressure vs. time for the reaction between A and B gas to form C gas. Gas A is present in excess.

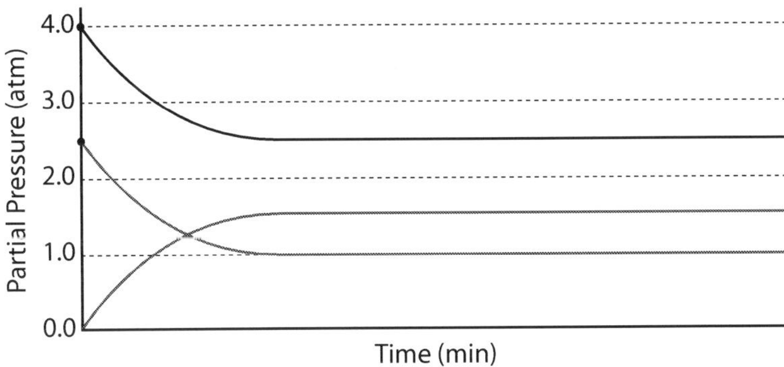

(a) Write a balanced chemical equation for the equilibrium in the question.

(b) Write the equilibrium expression K_p for the reaction.

(c) Calculate the numerical value for K_p for this reaction.

(d) Calculate the numerical value for K_c for this reaction.

22. In a container, 1.00 mol of N_2 and 3.00 mol of H_2 are mixed together to produce ammonia. At equilibrium, the total pressure of the system is 1.8×10^6 Pa and the mixture contains only 50% of the N_2 that was present originally. Calculate K_p for this reaction at this temperature.

23. A lab technician places 0.300 atm of SO_2, 0.400 atm O_2, and 0.020 atm of SO_3 into a 10.0 L bulb. Once equilibrium is established, the partial pressure of SO_3 is found to be 0.140 atm. What is the value of K_p for the reaction under these conditions?

24. $PCl_5(g)$ decomposes into $PCl_3(g)$ and $Cl_2(g)$. A pure sample of phosphorus pentachloride is placed into an evacuated 1.00 L glass bulb. The temperature remains constant while the pure sample decomposes as shown below:

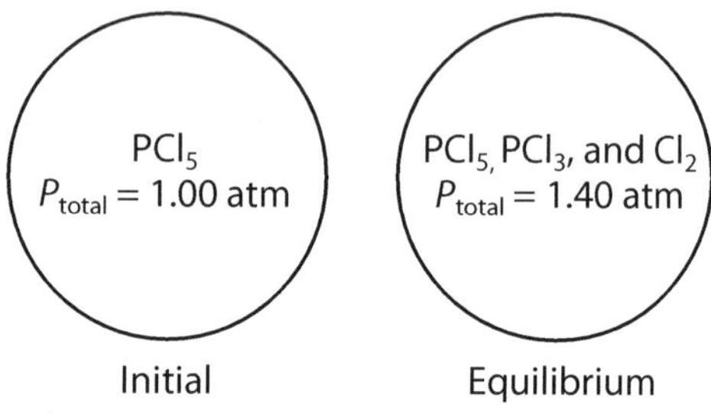

(a) Explain why the pressure increases in the container as the reaction reaches equilibrium.

(b) Determine the partial pressure of each gas when the system reaches equilibrium.

(c) Calculate K_p for the equilibrium system.

(d) If the decomposition were to go to completion, what would the total pressure be in the system?

2.6 Activity: Visualizing Equilibria

Question

How could you determine an equilibrium system's constant if you were able to count the number of molecules present at equilibrium?

Background

The amount of each reactant and product remains constant at equilibrium because each chemical is being produced at the same rate that it is being consumed. The diagrams below represent the interconversion of A (dark) molecules and B (light) molecules:

$$\text{A (dark)} \rightleftharpoons \text{B (light)}$$

Procedure

1. Each row of drawings represents a separate trial that results in equilibrium. Answer the questions below about the trials.

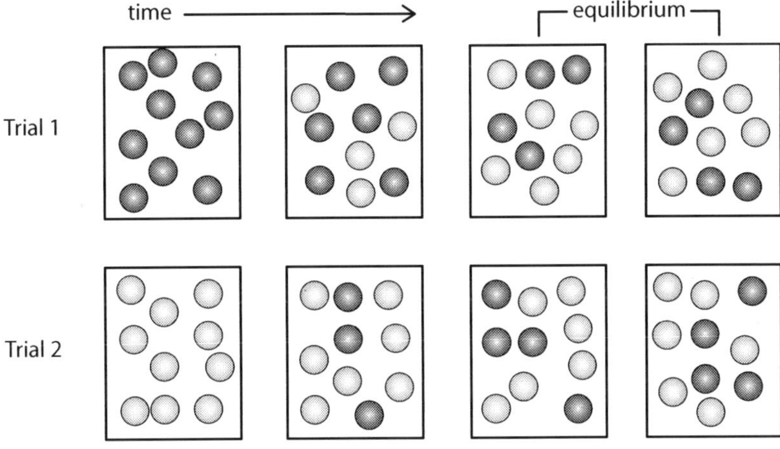

Results and Discussion

1. State a property of chemical equilibrium that is evident by observing trials 1 and 2.

2. What is the equilibrium constant for A $\rightleftharpoons$ B? The container could be any volume because the volumes cancel in this particular equilibrium expression.

3. In another trial, 20 A molecules and 50 B molecules were counted in a reaction vessel. How many A molecules will there be in the vessel when equilibrium is established?

4. After equilibrium was established in trial 2, the temperature was decreased. When equilibrium was restored, there were 7 A molecules and 3 B molecules in the container. State whether A $\rightleftharpoons$ B is exothermic or endothermic.

3 Thermodynamics

This chapter focuses on the following AP Big Idea from the College Board:

- Big Idea 5: The laws of thermodynamics describe the essential role of energy and explain and predict the direction of changes in matter.

By the end of this chapter, you should be able to do the following:

- Use representations and models to predict the sign and relative magnitude of the entropy change associated with chemical or physical processes
- Predict, either quantitatively or qualitatively, whether or not a physical or chemical process is thermodynamically favored by determination of the signs of both $\Delta H°$ and $\Delta S°$, and calculation or estimation of $\Delta G°$ when needed
- Determine whether a chemical or physical process is thermodynamically favorable by calculating the change in standard Gibbs free energy
- Explain why a thermodynamically favored chemical reaction may not produce large amounts of product based on consideration of both initial conditions and kinetic effects, or why a thermodynamically unfavored chemical reaction can produce large amounts of product for certain sets of initial conditions

By the end of this chapter, you should know the meaning of these **key terms**:

- endergonic
- exergonic
- Gibbs free energy
- microstates
- positional disorder
- second law of thermodynamics
- thermal disorder
- thermodynamically favorable
- third law of thermodynamics

Thermodynamics is the study of heat and temperature and their relation to energy and work. It includes concepts such as entropy and pressure.

Edvantage Science AP Chemistry 2

Chapter 3

Traffic Light Study Guide

Section	Page	I can ...	Red	Yellow	Green
3.1	182	State the *first law of thermodynamics*.	○	○	○
	183	State the *second law of thermodynamics*.	○	○	○
	183 - 184	Write the *Boltzmann equation* and state the *third law of thermodynamics*.	○	○	○
	184	State how a system's temperature affects its *thermal disorder* and its Δ thermal disorder when heat is added or removed.	○	○	○
	185 - 186	Calculate the entropy change and thus determine the spontaneity of a reaction, given the reactants' and products' *standard entropies (S°)*.	○	○	○
3.2	191 - 192	Provide the formula for the change of *Gibb's Free Energy (ΔG)* and relate a reaction's free energy to its spontaneity.	○	○	○
	192, 196	Predict the spontaneity of a reaction, given the signs of ΔH and ΔS. In cases where those signs are the same, relate spontaneity to temperature.	○	○	○
	193	Relate a reaction's change of Free Energy (ΔG) to the amount of recoverable energy it releases.	○	○	○
	193	State the value of ΔG for a reaction at equilibrium.	○	○	○
	194 – 195	Use the *Gibbs-Helmholtz Equation* to calculate a *Standard Free Energy Change (ΔG°)* at Standard Temperature.	○	○	○
	196	Use *Free Energies of Formation* to calculate a Standard Free Energy Change (ΔG°) at Standard Temperature.	○	○	○
	197 – 198	Use the *Gibbs-Helmholtz Equation* to calculate a Standard Free Energy Change (ΔG) at Non-Standard Temperatures.	○	○	○
3.3	205 - 206	Calculate the change of Free *Energy* (ΔG) for a reaction mixture with gaseous species at Non-Standard Pressures. Determine the direction the reaction will proceed to achieve equilibrium.	○	○	○
	207 - 209	Convert a Standard Free Energy change (ΔG°) into K_{eq} (and vice-versa).	○	○	○
	210	Draw diagrams showing how Free Energy changes during the course of exergonic and endergonic reactions at constant temperature.	○	○	○

For more support in AP Chemistry 2, go to edvantagescience.com

3.1 Entropy — A Quantitative Treatment

1. Predict the sign you would expect for $\Delta S°$ in each of the following processes. Give a short explanation of why you think it is (+) or (–). Do NOT do any calculations.
   (a) Blowing up a building

   (b) Organizing a stack of files in alphabetical order

   (c) $AgCl(s) \rightarrow Ag^+(aq) + Cl^-(aq)$

   (d) $2\,H_2(g) + O_2\,(g) \rightarrow 2\,H_2O(l)$

   (e) $Na(s) + ½\,Cl_2(g) \rightarrow NaCl(s)$

   (f) Removing medication from bottles and organizing the pills by the day in "blister packs"

2. Predict the sign of $\Delta S°$ you would expect for each of the following changes. Give a short explanation of why you think it is (+) or (–). Do NOT do any calculations.

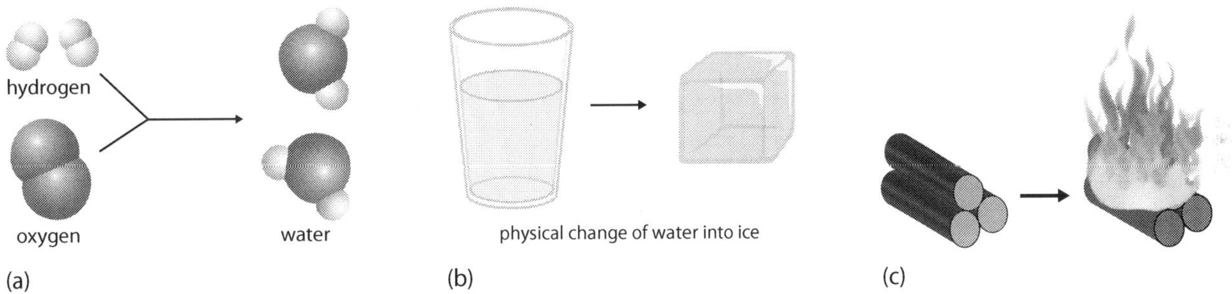

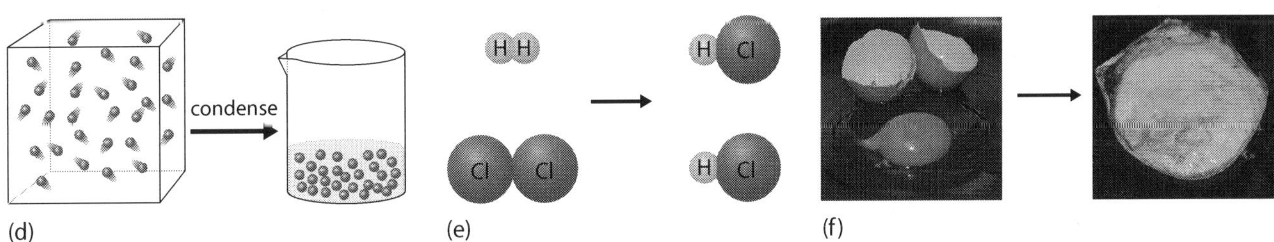

3. The boiling point of chloroform ($CHCl_3$) is 61.7° C. The enthalpy of vaporization is 31.4 kJ/mol. Calculate the entropy of vaporization. Does the sign for entropy of vaporization make sense? Explain.

4. (a) What is the normal boiling point for formic acid, HCOOH?
Given: $\Delta H_f^\circ = -424.72$ kJ/mol for liquid HCOOH and –379.1 kJ/mol for gaseous HCOOH
$S^\circ = 128.95$ J/mol K for liquid HCOOH and 251.0 J/mol K for gaseous HCOOH

(b) Based on the calculated boiling point, in what state does formic acid exist at room temperature? Explain.

5. The normal boiling point of water is 100.0°C, and its molar enthalpy of vaporization is 40.7 kJ/mol. What is the change in entropy in the system in J/K when 39.3 g of steam at 1 atm condenses to a liquid at the normal boiling point? Does the sign for the value you calculate make sense? Explain.

6. Iodine is an unusual element that sublimes under standard conditions. If the ΔS°_{subl} of iodine is 145 J/mol K and the ΔH°_{subl} of iodine is 62 kJ/mol, what is the standard sublimation temperature for iodine?

7. Consider the following addition reaction: $C_2H_2(g) + 2\,H_2(g) \rightarrow C_2H_6(g)$
The following data is known for this reaction:

Substance	S° (J/mol K)	ΔH_f (kJ/mol)
$C_2H_2(g)$	200.9	226.7
$H_2(g)$	130.7	0
$C_2H_6(g)$	????	–84.7

(a) If the value of ΔS° for the reaction is –232.7 J/mol K, calculate the value of S° for C_2H_6 gas.

(b) Calculate the enthalpy change ΔH° for the reaction.

(c) Assume that Boltzmann's equation applies when the system is in equilibrium. What is the temperature at this point (use the non-SI unit of °C)?

8. Consider the following reaction: $2\ H_2S(g) + SO_2(g) \rightarrow 3\ S(s) + 2\ H_2O(g)$
(a) Predict the sign of $\Delta S°$ for the reaction at 298 K. Explain the basis of your prediction.

(b) Calculate the actual value of $\Delta S°$ for the reaction. Assume the sulfur produced is the *rhombic* form. Does your calculation justify your prediction? Explain.

9. The combustion of methanol is described by the following equation:

$$2\ CH_3OH(l) + 3\ O_2(g) \rightarrow 4\ H_2O(l) + 2\ CO_2(g)$$

The value of $\Delta S°$ for this reaction is –38.6 cal/mol K at 25°C. One calorie is the energy required to warm 1 g of water by 1°C. One calorie is equivalent to 4.18 J.
Data collected for this reaction:

Reaction Species	ΔH°_f (kcal/mol) at SATP	$S°$ (cal/mol K) at SATP
$CH_3OH(l)$	–57.0	30.3
$H_2O(l)$	–68.3	16.7
$CO_2(g)$	–94.0	51.1

Calculate the standard absolute entropy $S°$ per mole of $O_2(g)$. Convert this value to units of J/mol K.

10. Use the values in Table A8 in the appendix to calculate $\Delta S°$ for each of the following equations. (It is important to use the values in the appendix because entropy values may differ slightly from one source to another. It is important to refer to the recommended source for reference values to ensure consistency in answers.)

(a) $H_2(g) + ½ O_2(g) \rightarrow H_2O(g)$

(b) $3 O_2(g) \rightarrow 2 O_3(g)$

(c) $CH_4(g) + 2 O_2(g) \rightarrow CO_2(g) + 2 H_2O(g)$

(d) $P_4O_{10}(s) + 6 H_2O(l) \rightarrow 4 H_3PO_4(s)$
(Given $S°$ for solid phosphoric acid = 110.54 J/mol K.)

(e) The complete combustion of octane in gasoline

3.2 Gibbs Free Energy

1. (a) What two factors, other than temperature, influence the spontaneity of a process?

   (b) Describe each factor.

   (c) What sign is associated with spontaneity for each factor?

2. Complete the following table for the equation: $\Delta G° = \Delta H° - T\Delta S°$.

Sign of $\Delta H°$	Sign of $\Delta S°$	Temperature	Sign of $\Delta G°$	Spontaneous /Non-Spontaneous
–	+	low		
–	+	high		
+	–	low		
+	–	high		
–	–		–	
+	+			spontaneous
–	–	high		
+	+		+	

3. Examine the representation of ice melting and water condensing on a glass of ice water. Consider circled areas A and B.
   Circle A:
   (i) What are the signs of $\Delta H°$ and $\Delta S°$ for this process? Explain your answers.

   (ii) Is this process spontaneous at all temperatures, only low temperatures, only high temperatures or never? Explain.

   Circle B:
   (i) What are the signs of $\Delta H°$ and $\Delta S°$ for this process? Explain your answers.

   (ii) Is this process spontaneous at all temperatures, only low temperatures, only high temperatures or never? Explain.

4. $\Delta H°$ is –196.1 kJ/mol$_{rxn}$ for the following representation of a reaction of $H_2O_2(l)$.

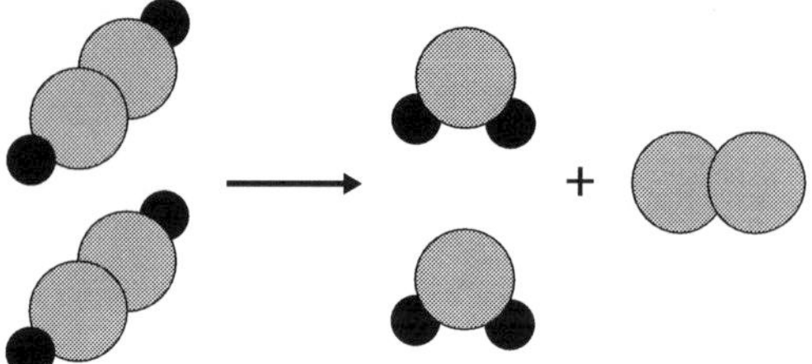

(a) What are the signs of $\Delta S°$ and $\Delta G°$ for the reaction? Explain.

(b) Is the process spontaneous at all temperatures, only low temperatures, only high temperatures or never? Explain.

5. (a) Use the representation below to produce a balanced chemical equation. Use the lowest possible whole number coefficients in your equation.

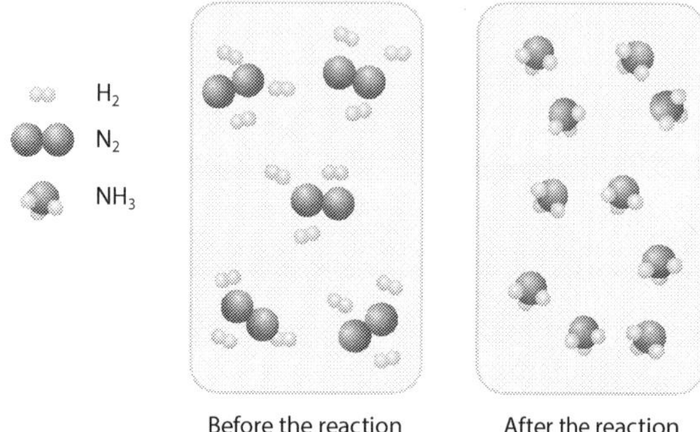

(b) Use Table A8 in the appendix to calculate $\Delta H°_{rxn}$ for the reaction. Show your work.

(c) Predict the *sign* of $\Delta S°_{rxn}$ for the reaction (do not calculate).

(d) Is this process spontaneous at all temperatures, only low temperatures, only high temperatures or never? Explain.

(e) Determine the temperature (in °C) at which the spontaneity of this reaction changes.

6. Shiny silver iodine crystals are deposited on the surface of ice placed into a test tube filled with purple iodine vapor.

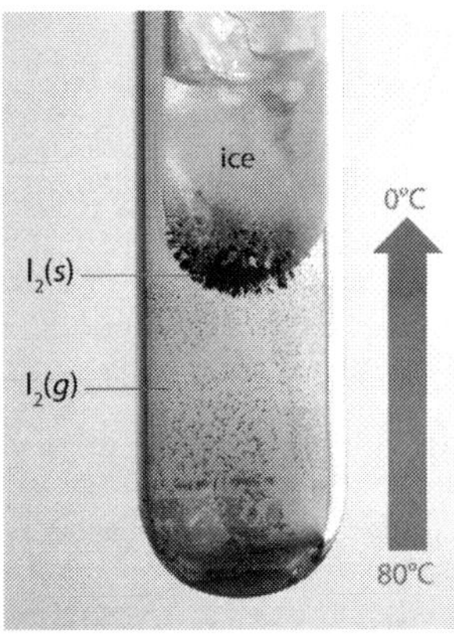

(a) Write a balanced chemical equation to describe the process pictured here.

(b) Use Table A8 in the appendix to calculate the sublimation temperature (same as the deposition temperature) for iodine.

7. Consider the following reaction: $2\ O_3(g) \rightarrow 3\ O_2(g)$. $\Delta H° = -285.4\ kJ/mol_{rxn}$.

(a) Predict the signs for $\Delta S°_{rxn}$ and $\Delta G°_{rxn}$ and the spontaneity of the reaction (no calculations required).

(b) Use values from Table A8 in the appendix to calculate $\Delta S°_{rxn}$ and $\Delta G°_{rxn}$ and to determine the accuracy of your prediction.

8. Calculate $\Delta G°_{rxn}$ for each of the following reactions using Table A8 in the appendix.

(a) $NH_3(g) + HCl(g) \rightarrow NH_4Cl(s)$

(b) $AgNO_3(aq) + NaI(aq) \rightarrow AgI(s) + NaNO_3(aq)$ (Hint: Use the net ionic equation.)

(c) $P_4O_{10}(s) + H_2O(l) \rightarrow H_3PO_4(l)$ (Hint: The reaction is unbalanced.)

9. Government requirements in the United States and Canada state that fuels should contain a "renewable" component. Fermentation of glucose isolated from a variety of garden products such as sugar cane, beets, and corn produces ethanol. Producers can add ethanol to gasoline to fulfill the renewable fuel requirement. Here is the fermentation reaction for glucose:

$C_6H_{12}O_6(s) \rightarrow 2\ C_2H_5OH(l) + 2\ CO_2(g)$

Calculate:

(a) $\Delta H°$

(b) $\Delta S°$

(c) $\Delta G°$

(d) Under what temperature conditions does this reaction occur spontaneously? Justify.

(e) How might this impact the economic feasibility of producing renewable fuels in this way?

10. In low concentrations, phosgene is a colorless to pale yellow cloud with the pleasant odor of freshly cut hay. In higher concentrations, phosgene becomes a choking agent toxic to the pulmonary system. Armies used phosgene to kill hundreds of people during the World War 1. Carbon monoxide and chlorine combine to form phosgene, $COCl_2(g)$.

    (a) Calculate $\Delta S°_{rxn}$ given that $\Delta H° = -220.$ kJ/mol$_{rxn}$ and $\Delta G° = -206$ kJ/mol$_{rxn}$ at 25 °C.

    (b) The (–)$\Delta G°$ value means the production of the war gas is spontaneous under SATP conditions. Considering the signs of $\Delta S°$ and $\Delta H°$, what temperature conditions should further favor the spontaneous production of phosgene?

    (c) Assuming the temperature effects on $\Delta S°$ and $\Delta H°$ are negligible, calculate $\Delta G°$ at 435°C. Is the reaction spontaneous at this higher temperature?

3.3 Pressure, Equilibrium, and Free Energy

1. Calculate $\Delta G°$ for the conversion of oxygen to ozone:
   $3\ O_2(g) \rightleftharpoons 2\ O_3(g)$ at 25°C given that $K = 2.50 \times 10^{-29}$

2. Consider the reaction: $MgCO_3(s) \rightleftharpoons MgO(s) + CO_2(g)$
   (a) Is the forward reaction spontaneous at room temperature (25°C)? Give a mathematical justification.

   (b) Is the reaction driven by enthalpy, entropy, both, or neither? Give a mathematical justification.

   (c) What is the value of K at 25°C?

   (d) At what temperature does the direction of the spontaneous reaction change?

   (e) Does high temperature make the reaction more or less spontaneous in the forward direction? Include a full explanation.

3. Methane, $CH_4(g)$, is the main component of natural gas. When the barrel of a Bunsen burner is wide open, more oxygen ($O_2(g)$) is available for the combustion of the methane. The products are entirely $CO_2(g)$ and $H_2O(g)$. When the barrel is nearly closed, the products are $CO_2(g)$ and some $H_2O(l)$.

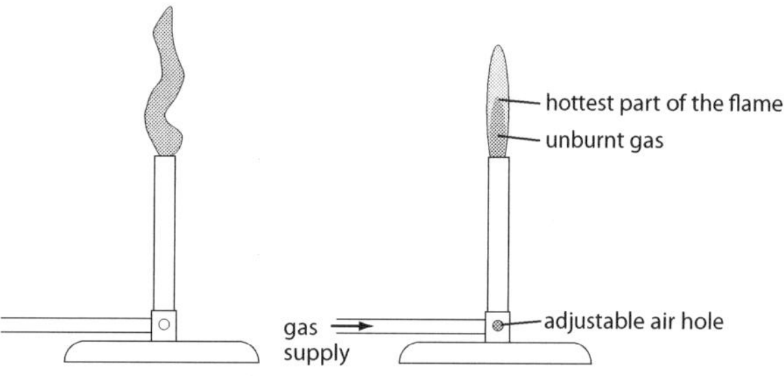

(a) Calculate $\Delta G°$ at 25°C for each reaction.

(b) Calculate K for each reaction.

(c) Which burner adjustment gives a hotter flame?

(d) Why does opening the barrel on the burner force a more complete combustion?

4. Use the reference values for $\Delta H_f°$ and $S°$ from Table A8 in the appendix to calculate $\Delta H°$, $\Delta S°$, and $\Delta G°$ for the reaction:

$CO(g) + H_2O(g) \rightleftharpoons CO_2(g) + H_2(g)$ at 25°C.

(a) $\Delta H°$ (Show all work completely.)

(b) $\Delta S°$ (Show all work completely.)

(c) $\Delta G°$ (Use the Gibbs-Helmholtz equation with a temperature of 25°C.)

(d) Calculate the equilibrium constant *K* for this reaction at 25°C.

(e) Calculate the equilibrium constant *K* for this reaction at 225°C.

(f) Using your answers to parts (d) and (e), determine whether this reaction is exo- or endothermic? Justify your answer. Does this response agree with the answer to part (a)?

5. Consider what each of the following graphs represent.

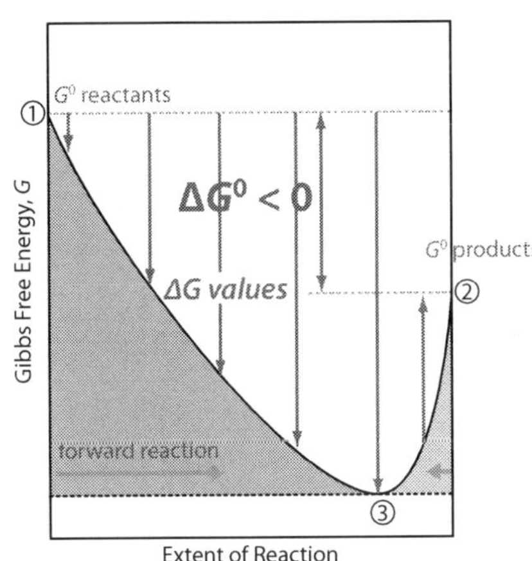

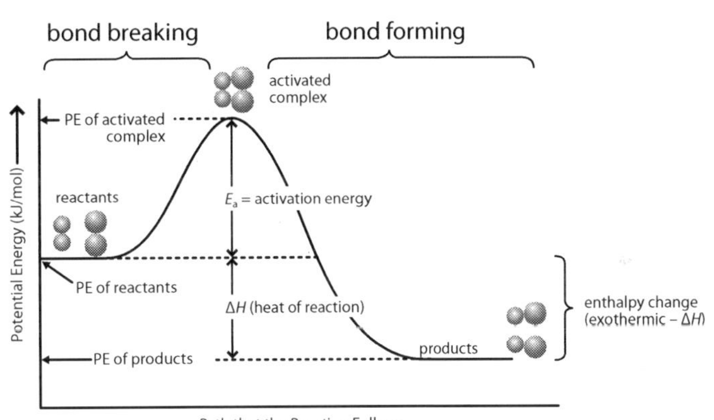

(a) How are the graphs similar? Be specific.

(b) How are the graphs different? Be specific.

6. Consider the following representations of a physical and a chemical change. Answer each question for A and B.

A. A physical change

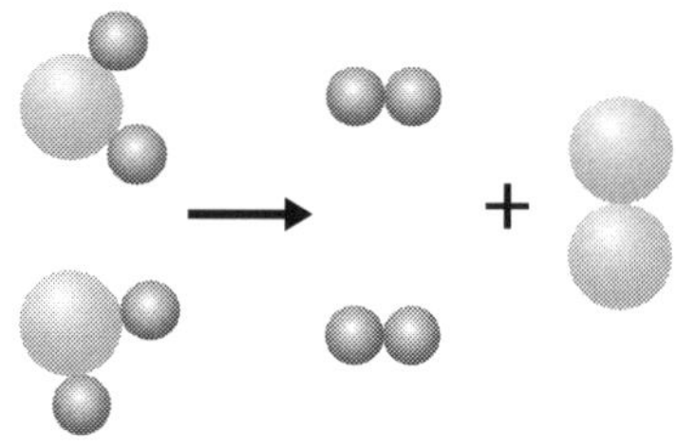

B. A chemical change

(a) What is the sign of $\Delta H°$?

(b) What is the sign of $\Delta S°$?

(c) How does the sign of $\Delta G°$ vary with temperature?

7. Consider the following reaction:

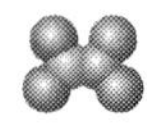 

$N_2O_4(g) \rightleftharpoons 2\ NO_2(g)$

(a) Calculate $\Delta G°$.

(b) Examine the following molecular representation. Assume each molecule exerts a partial pressure of 0.010 atm at 25°C. Calculate ΔG.

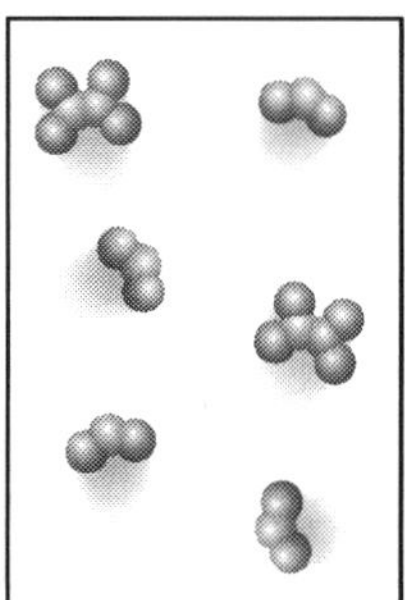

(c) In general, how would the representation change if the system were to achieve equilibrium?

8. Consider the following reaction at 25°C.

$$2\,NO(g) + O_2(g) \rightleftharpoons 2\,NO_2(g) \quad \Delta G^\circ = -71.2 \text{ kJ/mol}_{rxn}$$

(a) Calculate ΔG under the following conditions:

$P_{NO} = 0.0500$ atm $\quad P_{O_2} = 0.0500$ atm $\quad P_{NO_2} = 0.100$ atm

(b) Is the reaction more or less spontaneous under these pressure conditions?

9. (a) Given $\Delta G = -5.44$ kJ/mol, calculate ΔG at 298 K for the reaction $2\,ICl(g) \rightleftharpoons I_2(g) + Cl_2(g)$ in a mixture containing the following partial pressures:

$P_{ICl} = 2.0$ atm $\quad P_{I_2} = 0.0020$ atm $\quad P_{Cl_2} = 0.0020$ atm

(Remember: I_2 is normally a solid under standard conditions.)

(b) Is this reaction more or less spontaneous under these conditions than under standard conditions?

10. At 25°C, acetic acid, CH_3COOH, ionizes in water to form hydrogen and acetate ions. The acid is quite weak and has a small equilibrium constant, K_a, of 1.8 x 10^{-5}. $CH_3COOH(aq) \rightleftharpoons H^+(aq) + CH_3COO^-(aq)$

(a) Calculate $\Delta G°$ for the ionization of acetic acid.

(b) Calculate ΔG for the reaction if $[CH_3COOH]$ = 0.10 mol/L, $[H^+]$ = 9.5 x 10^{-5} mol/L, and $[CH_3COO^-]$ = 9.5 x 10^{-5} mol/L.

(c) Compare the spontaneity of ionization under the conditions in part (b) to those under standard conditions.

4 Solubility Equilibrium

This chapter focuses on the following AP Big Idea from the College Board:

- Big Idea 6: Any bond or intermolecular attraction that can be formed can be broken. These two processes are in a dynamic competition, sensitive to initial conditions and external perturbations.

By the end of this chapter, you should be able to do the following:

- Determine the solubility of a compound in aqueous solution
- Describe a saturated solution as an equilibrium system
- Determine the concentration of ions in a solution
- Determine the relative solubility of a substance, given solubility tables
- Apply solubility rules to analyze the composition of solutions
- Formulate equilibrium constant expressions for various saturated solutions
- Perform calculations involving solubility equilibrium concepts
- Devise a method for determining the concentration of a specific ion

By the end of this chapter, you should know the meaning of these **key terms**:

- aqueous solution
- common ion
- complete ionic equation
- dissociation equation
- electrical conductivity
- formula equation
- hard water
- ionic solution
- K_{sp}
- molecular solution
- net ionic equation
- precipitate
- relative solubility
- saturated solution
- solubility equilibrium

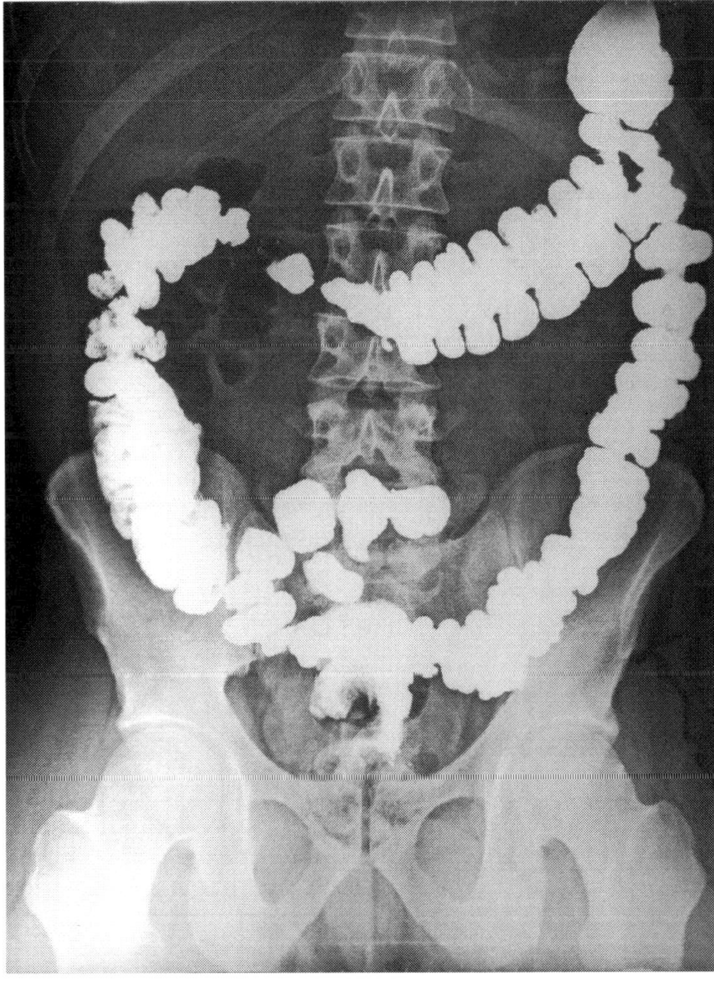

A patient must ingest a solution of barium sulfate for the large intestine (shown here) to be visible on an X-ray. The small solubility product, or K_{sp}, of $BaSO_4$ means humans can safely ingest the suspension.

Edvantage Science AP Chemistry 2

Chapter 4

Traffic Light Study Guide

Section	Page	I can ...	Red	Yellow	Green
4.1	218 - 220	Classify solutes as non-, weak, or strong *electrolytes*.	○	○	○
	220	Write *dissociation equations* for ionic solids.	○	○	○
	221	Calculate the *molarity* of a solution, given how it was prepared.	○	○	○
	221	Relate ion concentrations to the concentration of their parent compound and vice-versa.	○	○	○
	222	Calculate the resulting ion concentrations when a solution is diluted by adding water or by mixing it with another solution(s).	○	○	○
	223	Define *solubility*.	○	○	○
	223	Convert g/mL to Molarity and vice-versa.	○	○	○
	224	Describe the chemical equilibrium that exists in *saturated* solutions of ionic solids.	○	○	○
4.2	228 - 229	Use the *Solubility Table* to determine whether an ionic solid is *soluble* or has *low solubility*.	○	○	○
	230	Write the *formula equation*, *complete ionic equation*, and *net ionic equation* for a *precipitation reaction*.	○	○	○
	230 - 232	State 3 techniques for identifying ions in solution. Identify what ions might be present in a solution from the results of precipitation trials, e.g. precipitates with SO_4^{2-} but not with OH^-.	○	○	○
	232 - 233	Devise a *selective precipitation* scheme to separate different types of ions from solution (e.g. SO_4^{2-} from S^{2-}) by precipitating them one at a time.	○	○	○
	234	Describe a technique that may be used to identify precipitates.	○	○	○
	235	Describe possible causes of, harms of, and treatments for *hard water*.	○	○	○
4.3	241 – 242	Define the *solubility product constant* (K_{sp}).	○	○	○
	242 – 243	Determine the K_{sp} of a compound from its solubility.	○	○	○
	245 - 246	Determine the solubility of a compound from its K_{sp}.	○	○	○
4.4	251 – 252	Determine whether a precipitate will form from a solution's ion concentrations.	○	○	○
	253 – 254	Calculate the maximum concentration of any ion that can coexist in a solution containing known concentrations of other ions.	○	○	○
	255	Describe and explain the *common ion effect*.	○	○	○
	256 - 257	Calculate the solubility of a compound in a solution containing a common ion.	○	○	○

4.1 The Concept of Solubility

1. Give three examples for each of the following:
   (a) strong electrolytes

   (b) non-electrolytes

2. Compare the electrical conductivity of 1.0 M $HClO_4$ to that of 1.0 M H_3PO_4. Explain your reasoning.

3. Write dissociation equations for the following in aqueous solution. Ensure that your equations are balanced for both number of atoms and charge.

   (a) magnesium perchlorate

   (b) calcium dichromate

   (c) copper(II) acetate

   (d) manganese(II) thiocyanate

   (e) aluminum binoxalate

   (f) barium hydroxide octahydrate

4. Barium sulfate is used in medicine as a radiopaque contrast material. Patients drink a suspension of barium sulfate to coat their gastrointestinal tract. The surface of the tissue being studied is then highly visible under X-ray or CT scan. Radiologists can better see disease or trauma internally using this method. What is the molar solubility of barium sulfate if a saturated solution contains 0.0012 g dissolved in 500. mL of solution?

5. Calcium carbonate is used to treat calcium deficiencies in the body. Your body needs calcium to build and maintain healthy bones. What mass of calcium carbonate is required to produce 250. mL of solution with a calcium ion concentration of 7.1×10^{-5} M ?

6. Sodium dichromate is used in the production of chromic acid; a common etching agent. Calculate the concentration of each ion in a solution of sodium dichromate prepared by dissolving 0.50 g in 150. mL of solution.

7. Solutions of magnesium chloride and sodium chloride are mixed to make brine commonly used to keep roads from becoming slippery because of ice. The brine solution lowers the freezing point of water by up to 10°C. A brine solution is made by mixing 60. L of 5.0 M sodium chloride with 30. L of 2.4 M magnesium chloride. Calculate the concentration of each ion in this solution.

8. Describe how you would prepare 1.0 L of a saturated solution of sodium chloride.

9. Write the equation for the equilibrium present in saturated solutions of the following:
   (a) silver bromate

   (b) aluminum chromate

   (c) magnesium hydroxide

   (d) lead(II) sulfate

   (e) copper(II) phosphate

4.1 Activity: A Solubility Crossword

Question

How can you construct a crossword to define vocabulary terms?

Background

Chemists use very precise vocabulary to describe concepts. A solid understanding of the meaning of these words is essential to understanding the concepts.

Procedure

1. Construct a crossword puzzle containing the following vocabulary terms:

anion	ionization	soluble
cation	molarity	solute
conductivity	molecular	solution
dissociation	precipitate	solvent
electrolyte	saturated	unsaturated
ionic	solubility	

2. Your clue for each term must be in your own words.

Results and Discussion

1. Exchange your crossword with your partners.
2. Complete your partner's crossword.
3. Were there terms that you found difficult to define? If they were, compile a list of these terms separately, and for each, identify examples that illustrate the meaning of the term.

4.2 Qualitative Analysis — Identifying Unknown Ions

1. Classify the following solutes as soluble or low solubility according to the solubility table (Table 4.2.1):
   (a) Rb_2SO_3

   (b) Al_2S_3

   (c) CuI

   (d) ammonium sulfate

   (e) chromium(III) nitrate

   (f) potassium oxalate

2. According to the solubility table, silver sulfate has a low solubility. In a saturated solution of silver sulfate, are silver and sulfate ions present in solution? Explain.

3. The solubility of silver acetate is 11.1 g/L at 25°C. According to the solubility table, would silver acetate be classified as being soluble or of low solubility?

4. Describe the difference between a formula equation, a complete ionic equation, and a net ionic equation. How are they similar? Different?

5. What is a spectator ion? Give an example of a cation and an anion that are common spectator ions in precipitate reactions.

6. Write a balanced formula equation, complete ionic equation, and net ionic equation for each of the following reactions:

   (a) $(NH_4)_2S(aq) + FeSO_4(aq) \rightarrow$

   (b) $H_2SO_3(aq) + CaCl_2(aq) \rightarrow$

   (c) copper(II) sulfate and calcium sulfide →

7. Explain why it would be difficult to separate the ions Na^+ and K^+ in solution using precipitation.

8. A solution contains Cr^{3+}, Ca^{2+}, and Mg^{2+} ions. Describe a method to remove each ion individually from solution. Be sure to state the compound you would add and how you would remove the precipitate from solution. For each reaction that occurs, write a net ionic equation.

9. A solution contains PO_4^{3-}, Cl^-, and S^{2-} ions. Describe a method to remove each ion individually from solution. Be sure to state the compound you would add and how you would remove the precipitate from solution. For each reaction that occurs, write a net ionic equation.

10. Why are compounds containing nitrates used to test for anions?

11. Give two examples where re-dissolving is necessary to separate two precipitates.

12. A solution of Na_2CO_3 is added to a solution of $AgNO_3$.
   (a) Write the net ionic equation for this reaction.

   (b) Two different reagents will dissolve the precipitate formed. Write a net ionic equation for each reaction in which the precipitate dissolves.

13. (a) Define *hard water* and *scale*.

   (b) Scale can be removed by adding a solution of HCl to the water. Write a formula equation, complete ionic equation, and net ionic equation for this reaction.

   (c) Suggest a substance that could be added to water to remove both Ca^{2+} and Mg^{2+} from solution.

   (d) Explain why adding a water softener to your washing machine when doing laundry improves the cleaning job on your clothes.

4.2 Activity: Using Titration to Calculate the Unknown $[Cl^-]$ In A Sample of Seawater

Question

What is the concentration of Cl^- in seawater?

Background

Titration is an analytical method used to determine the unknown amount of a substance in a sample by reacting it with a measured amount of another substance. You will become more familiar with titration in the acid-base and redox chapters later in this textbook.

Seawater contains a significant amount of salts, largely sodium chloride. In this activity, a sample of seawater is titrated against a standardized solution of silver nitrate. The silver ions cause the chloride ions in the seawater to form a white precipitate. The concentration of chloride ion can be determined by measuring the amount of silver ions required to completely precipitate out the chloride ion. An indicator of potassium chromate is used. When almost all of the chloride ions in the sample have precipitated, any added silver ion will react with the chromate ion, causing a red precipitate to form. The equivalence point is reached once the solution begins to turn reddish.

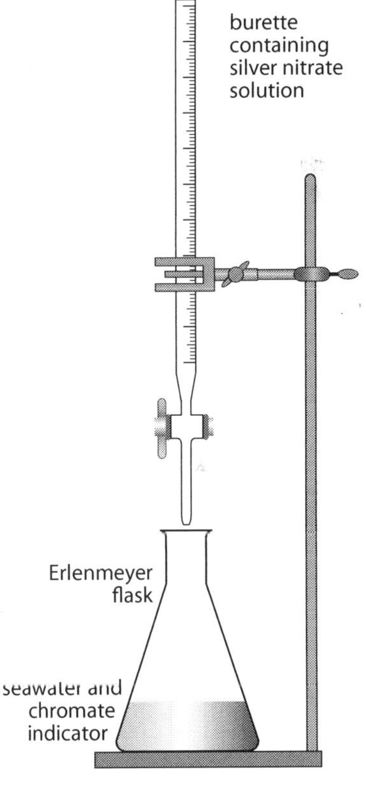

Procedure

1. A 25.0 mL sample of seawater was diluted to 250. mL. From this diluted solution, a 25.0 mL sample was measured out and placed in the Erlenmeyer flask.
2. A few drops of potassium chromate were added to the flask to act as an indicator.
3. A burette was filled with 0.100 M silver nitrate solution. An initial burette reading was taken. The silver nitrate solution was slowly added to the flask. A white precipitate formed. After a few more drops of silver nitrate were added, the precipitate turned a reddish color. At this point, no more silver nitrate was added. A final burette reading was recorded.
4. Procedure steps 1 to 3 were repeated in two more trials, and the data below was recorded.

	Trial 1	Trial 2	Trial 3
Initial burette reading (mL)	0.00	14.70	28.60
Final burette reading (mL)	14.70	28.60	42.35
Volume $AgNO_3$ added (mL)			
Average volume $AgNO_3$ used (mL)			

5. Complete the data table above by subtracting the initial volume from the final volume in each trial to determine the volume of silver nitrate added.
6. The average volume of silver nitrate added is calculated by taking the average of the closest two trials. Calculate the average volume of silver nitrate added, and record it in the data table.

Results and Discussion

1. Write a balanced net ionic equation that represents the reaction between silver ion and chloride ion.

2. Calculate the moles of silver nitrate reacted in the titration using the average volume and concentration of the silver nitrate.

3. Using the mole ratio from the balanced net ionic equation, calculate the moles of chloride ion present in the sample.

4. Using the volume of the *diluted* sample and the moles of chloride calculated above, calculate the concentration of chloride ion in the diluted sample.

5. Calculate the concentration of chloride ion in the original sample of seawater.

6. The level of salt in seawater varies across the planet. The average amount of chloride ion in seawater is 21.2 g/L. How does your sample compare?

7. Silver ions will form a precipitate with both chloride and chromate ions. Use a reference book to look up the solubility of $AgCl$ and Ag_2CrO_4. Calculate the concentration of Ag^+ in a saturated solution of each. Use this information to explain why $AgCl$ precipitates before Ag_2CrO_4.

4.3 The Solubility Product Constant K_{sp}

1. Write equilibrium equations and the corresponding K_{sp} expressions for each of the following solutes in saturated aqueous solution.

   (a) $Al(OH)_3$

   (b) $Cd_3(AsO_4)_2$

   (c) $BaMoO_4$

   (d) calcium sulfate

   (e) lead(II) iodate

   (f) silver carbonate

2. Consider a saturated solution of $BaSO_3$.
   (a) Write the equation that represents the equilibrium in the solution.

   (b) Explain the difference between the solubility and the solubility product constant of $BaSO_3$.

3. A saturated solution of $ZnCO_3$ was prepared by adding excess solid $ZnCO_3$ to water. The solution was analyzed and found to contain $[Zn^{2+}] = 1.1 \times 10^{-5}$ M. What is the K_{sp} for $ZnCO_3$?

4. When a student evaporated 250. mL of a saturated solution of silver phosphate, 0.0045 g of solute remained. Calculate the K_{sp} for silver phosphate.

5. Gypsum is used in drywall and plaster, and occurs naturally in alabaster. It has the formula $CaSO_4 \cdot 2\,H_2O$ and its K_{sp} is 9.1×10^{-6}. What mass of gypsum is present in 500. mL of saturated solution?

6. Naturally occurring limestone contains two forms of $CaCO_3$ called calcite and aragonite. They differ in their crystal structure. High-grade calcite crystals were used in World War II for gun sights, especially in anti-aircraft weaponry. Aragonite is used in jewelry and glassmaking. Using the following K_{sp} values, calculate the solubility of each in g/L.
   (a) K_{sp} calcite $= 3.4 \times 10^{-9}$

   (b) K_{sp} aragonite $= 6.0 \times 10^{-9}$

7. Lead(II) arsenate, $Pb_3(AsO_4)_2$, was commonly used as an insecticide, especially against codling moths. Because of the toxic nature of lead compounds, it was banned in the 1980s. It has a solubility of 3.0×10^{-5} g/L. Calculate the K_{sp} for lead(II) arsenate.

8. A student compares the K_{sp} values of cadmium carbonate ($K_{sp} = 1.0 \times 10^{-12}$) and cadmium hydroxide ($K_{sp} = 7.2 \times 10^{-15}$) and concludes that the solubility of cadmium carbonate is greater than the solubility of cadmium hydroxide. Do you agree or disagree? Support your answer with appropriate calculations.

9. A titration was carried out to determine the unknown concentration of Cl^- ion in solution. The standard solution was $AgNO_3$ and an indicator of K_2CrO_4 was used. The equivalence point was reached when the solution turned the red color of Ag_2CrO_4, signaling that virtually all of the Cl^- ions had been used up. Explain why a precipitate of AgCl formed before a precipitate of Ag_2CrO_4. Use data from the K_{sp} table provided in this section.

10. Silver carbonate is used as an antibacterial agent in the production of concrete. What mass of silver carbonate must be dissolved to produce 2.5 L of saturated solution?

4.3 Activity: Experimentally Determining the K_{sp} of $CaCO_3$

Question

What is the K_{sp} of $CaCO_3$?

Background

The K_{sp} of a substance is temperature dependent. Your task is to design an experiment to determine the K_{sp} of calcium carbonate at a predetermined temperature.

Procedure

1. Choose a temperature between 10°C and 30°C. Design an experiment to determine the K_{sp} of calcium carbonate at that temperature. Your experiment should include:
   - a list of reagents
   - a list of apparatus
   - a detailed step-by-step procedure
   - appropriate data tables

Results and Discussion

1. Describe how you would analyze the data and perform calculations to determine the K_{sp}.

2. What would be some sources of error?

3. Compare your procedure to that of another group. Was their procedure the same?

4.4 Precipitation Formation and the Solubility Product K_{sp}

1. The following solutions were mixed together. Write the equilibrium equation for the precipitate that forms and its K_{sp} expression.
   (a) $FeCl_2$ and Na_2S

   (b) $Sr(OH)_2$ and $MgBr_2$

   (c) silver nitrate and ammonium chromate

2. A student mixed equal volumes of 0.2 M solutions of sulfuric acid and calcium chloride together.
   (a) What precipitate forms?

   (b) Write an equation for the equilibrium present and the K_{sp} expression.

   (c) In the resulting solution, does $[SO_4^{2-}] = [Ca^{2+}]$? Explain.

3. What is the maximum $[Pb^{2+}]$ that can exist in 0.015 M $CuSO_4$?

4. Kidney stones are crystals of calcium oxalate that form in the kidney, ureter, or bladder. Small kidney stones are passed out of the body easily, but larger kidney stones may block the ureter causing severe pain. If the $[Ca^{2+}]$ in blood plasma is 5×10^{-3} M, what $[C_2O_4^{2-}]$ must be present to form a kidney stone?

5. What is the maximum $[CO_3^{2-}]$ that can exist in a saturated solution of AgBr?

6. A 100.0 mL sample of seawater was tested by adding one drop (0.2 mL) of 0.20 M silver nitrate. What mass of NaCl is present in the seawater to form a precipitate?

7. Does a precipitate form when 2.5 mL of 0.055 M $Sr(NO_3)_2$ is added to 1.5 L of 0.011 M $ZnSO_4$? Justify your answer with calculations.

8. Does a precipitate form when 0.068 g of lead(II) nitrate is added to 2.0 L of 0.080 M NaCl? Justify your answer with calculations. (Assume no volume change.)

9. The addition of Ag^+ to a solution containing Cl^- and I^- will cause precipitates of both AgCl and AgI to form. Because AgCl and AgI have quite different K_{sp} values, you can use this information to separate Cl^- from I^- in solution by carefully manipulating the $[Ag^+]$ so that only one of Cl^- or I^- precipitates at a time. Consider a solution containing 0.020 M Cl^- and 0.020 M I^-. Solid silver nitrate is slowly added without changing the overall volume of solution.

(a) Write the equilibrium equation for each precipitate that forms.

(b) Beside each equilibrium equation, write the corresponding K_{sp} expression and value from your K_{sp} table.

(c) Based on the K_{sp} values, which precipitate will form first?

(d) Calculate the $[Ag^+]$ required just to start precipitation of the first precipitate.

(e) Calculate the $[Ag^+]$ required just to start precipitation of the second precipitate.

(f) State the range of $[Ag^+]$ required to precipitate I^- but not Cl^-.

(g) What $[I^-]$ remains in solution just before the formation of AgCl?

(h) What percentage of I^- is precipitated out before the AgCl starts to precipitate?

10. Washing soda, $Na_2CO_3 \cdot 10\ H_2O$ is used to treat hard water containing Ca^{2+} and Mg^{2+}. A 1.0 L sample contained 12 mg of Mg^{2+}. What mass of washing soda is required to precipitate out the Mg^{2+}?

11. List two substances that, when added to water, that would decrease the solubility of lead(II) iodate. Explain each.

12. Explain why $BaSO_4$ is less soluble in a solution of Na_2SO_4 than in water.

13. Is iron(III) hydroxide more or less soluble in water than in 0.1 M HCl? Explain.

14. An aqueous suspension of $BaSO_4$ is used as a contrast agent to improve the quality of intestinal X-rays. The patient drinks a suspension of $BaSO_4$. However, Ba^{2+} is toxic, so the $BaSO_4$ is dissolved in a solution of 0.10 M Na_2SO_4.
(a) Calculate the maximum mass of $BaSO_4$ that can be dissolved in 200. mL of water. (Assume no volume change.)

(b) Calculate the maximum mass of $BaSO_4$ that can be dissolved in 200. mL of 0.10 M Na_2SO_4 without forming a precipitate.

4.4 Activity: Experimentally Determining the K_{sp} Of Copper(II) Iodate

Question
What is the approximate value of K_{sp} for copper(II) iodate?

Background
A TIP calculation can be used to determine if a precipitate will form. If TIP > K_{sp}, a precipitate forms. If TIP < K_{sp}, no precipitate forms. Five different dilutions of copper(II) nitrate and sodium iodate were prepared and mixed together. By observing which mixed solutions contained a precipitate, information about the K_{sp} can be deduced.

Procedure:
1. Five different dilutions of copper(II) nitrate and sodium iodate were prepared as shown in the data table below. The given volume of each solution was mixed together with water and the formation of a precipitate was noted. Answer the questions below.

	Mixture 1	Mixture 2	Mixture 3	Mixture 4	Mixture 5
Volume 0.010 M $Cu(NO_3)_2$ (mL)	10.0	8.0	6.0	4.0	2.0
Volume 0.020 M $NaIO_3$ (mL)	10.0	8.0	6.0	4.0	2.0
Volume water added (mL)	0.0	4.0	8.0	12.0	16.0
Observation	precipitate	precipitate	precipitate	no precipitate	no precipitate

Results and Discussion
1. Write balanced formula, complete ionic, and net ionic equations for this reaction.

2. Calculate the $[Cu^{2+}]$ in each of the mixtures.

3. Calculate the $[IO_3^-]$ in each of the mixtures.

4. Write the equation for the equilibrium involving the precipitate, and the K_{sp} expression.

5. Calculate a TIP value for each mixture.

6. State the K_{sp} as a range of values from this data.

7. Compare your range to the stated K_{sp} value on the K_{sp} table (Table 4.3.1).

4.4 Data Tables

Table 4.2.1 *Solubility of Common Compounds in Water*

Note: In this table, soluble means > 0.1 mol/L at 25°C.

Negative Ions (Anions)	Positive Ions (Cations)	Solubility of Compounds
All	Alkali ions: Li^+, Na^+, K^+, Rb^+, Cs^+, Fr^+	Soluble
All	Hydrogen ion: H^+	Soluble
All	Ammonium ion: NH_4^+	Soluble
Nitrate: NO_3^-	All	Soluble
Chloride: Cl^- Or Bromide: Br^- Or Iodide: I^-	All others	Soluble
	Ag^+, Pb^{2+}, Cu^+	Low solubility
Sulfate: SO_4^{2-}	All others	Soluble
	Ag^+, Ca^{2+}, Sr^{2+}, Ba^{2+}, Pb^{2+}	Low solubility
Sulfide: S^{2-}	Alkali ions, H^+, NH_4^+, Be^{2+}, Mg^{2+}, Ca^{2+}, Sr^{2+}, Ba^{2+}	Soluble
	All others	Low solubility
Hydroxide: OH^-	Alkali ions, H^+, NH_4^+, Sr^{2+}	Soluble
	All others	Low solubility
Phosphate: PO_4^{3-} Or Carbonate: CO_3^{2-} Or Sulfite: SO_3^{2-}	Alkali ions, H^+, NH_4^+	Soluble
	All others	Low solubility

Table 4.3.1 *Solubility Product Constants at 25°C*

Name	Formula	K_{sp}
Barium carbonate	$BaCO_3$	2.6×10^{-9}
Barium chromate	$BaCrO_4$	1.2×10^{-10}
Barium sulfate	$BaSO_4$	1.1×10^{-10}
Calcium carbonate	$CaCO_3$	5.0×10^{-9}
Calcium oxalate	CaC_2O_4	2.3×10^{-9}
Calcium sulfate	$CaSO_4$	7.1×10^{-5}
Copper(I) iodide	CuI	1.3×10^{-12}
Copper(II) iodate	$Cu(IO_3)_2$	6.9×10^{-8}
Copper(II) sulfide	CuS	6.0×10^{-37}
Iron(II) hydroxide	$Fe(OH)_2$	4.9×10^{-17}
Iron(II) sulfide	FeS	6.0×10^{-19}
Iron(III) hydroxide	$Fe(OH)_3$	2.6×10^{-39}
Lead(II) bromide	$PbBr_2$	6.6×10^{-6}
Lead(II) chloride	$PbCl_2$	1.2×10^{-5}
Lead(II) iodate	$Pb(IO_3)_2$	3.7×10^{-13}
Lead(II) iodide	PbI_2	8.5×10^{-9}
Lead(II) sulfate	$PbSO_4$	1.8×10^{-8}
Magnesium carbonate	$MgCO_3$	6.8×10^{-6}
Magnesium hydroxide	$Mg(OH)_2$	5.6×10^{-12}
Silver bromate	$AgBrO_3$	5.3×10^{-5}
Silver bromide	$AgBr$	5.4×10^{-13}
Silver carbonate	Ag_2CO_3	8.5×10^{-12}
Silver chloride	$AgCl$	1.8×10^{-10}
Silver chromate	Ag_2CrO_4	1.1×10^{-12}
Silver iodate	$AgIO_3$	3.2×10^{-8}
Silver iodide	AgI	8.5×10^{-17}
Strontium carbonate	$SrCO_3$	5.6×10^{-10}
Strontium fluoride	SrF_2	4.3×10^{-9}
Strontium sulfate	$SrSO_4$	3.4×10^{-7}
Zinc sulfide	ZnS	2.0×10^{-25}

5 Acid-Base Equilibrium

This chapter focuses on the following AP Big Ideas from the College Board:

- Big Idea 3: Changes in matter involve the rearrangement and/or reorganization of atoms and/or the transfer of electrons.
- Big Idea 6: Any bond or intermolecular attraction that can be formed can be broken. These two processes are in a dynamic competition, sensitive to initial conditions and external perturbations.

By the end of this chapter, you should be able to do the following:

- Identify acids and bases through experimentation
- Identify various models for representing acids and bases
- Analyze balanced equations representing the reaction of acids or bases with water
- Classify an acid or base in solution as either weak or strong, with reference to its electrical conductivity
- Analyze the equilibria that exist in weak acid or weak base systems
- Identify chemical species that are amphiprotic
- Analyze the equilibrium that exists in water
- Perform calculations relating pH, pOH, $[H_3O^+]$, and $[OH^-]$
- Explain the significance of the K_a and K_b equilibrium expressions
- Perform calculations involving K_a and K_b

By the end of this chapter, you should know the meaning of these **key terms**:

- acid
- acid ionization constant (K_a)
- amphiprotic
- Arrhenius
- base
- base ionization constant (K_b)
- Brønsted-Lowry
- conjugate acid-base pair
- electrical conductivity
- ion product constant
- mass action expression
- pH
- pK_w
- pOH
- polarized
- strong acid
- strong base
- water ionization constant (K_w)
- weak acid
- weak base

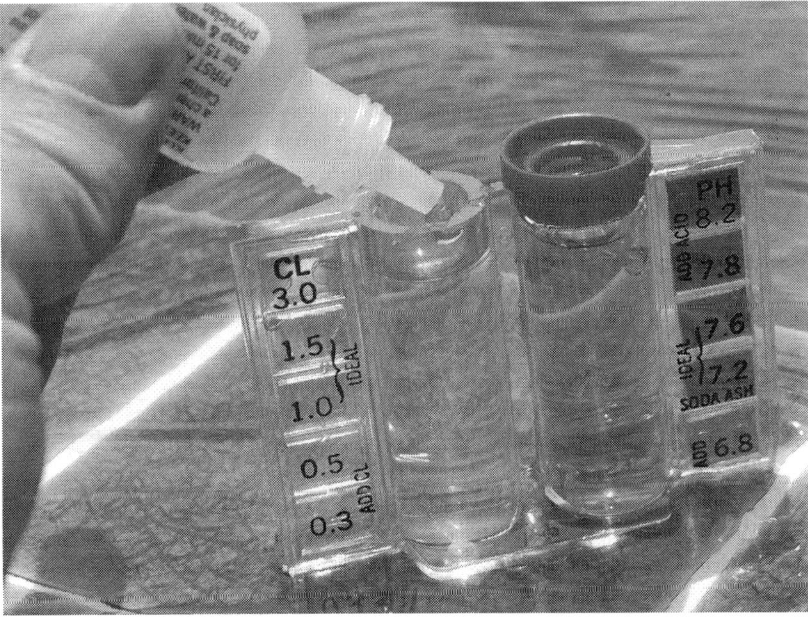

Testing swimming pool water involves acid-base interactions.

Edvantage Science AP Chemistry 2

Chapter 5

Traffic Light Study Guide

Section	Page	I can …	Red	Yellow	Green
5.1	264	Define and provide an example of an *Arrhenius acid* and an *Arrhenius base.*	○	○	○
	264	Determine the products of an Arrhenius acid-base reaction.	○	○	○
	265 – 266	Define and provide an example of a *Brønsted-Lowry acid* and a *Brønsted-Lowry base.*	○	○	○
	266 – 267	Determine the products of a Brønsted-Lowry acid-base reaction and identify its *conjugate acid-base pairs.*	○	○	○
	267	Determine a Brønsted-Lowry acid's conjugate base (and vice-versa).	○	○	○
	268	Define and provide an example of an *amphiprotic* species.	○	○	○
5.2	273 – 274	Define and provide an example of a *strong acid* and a *weak acid.*	○	○	○
	274	Define and provide an example of a *strong Brønsted-Lowry base* and a *weak Brønsted-Lowry base.*	○	○	○
	275	Write the *acid ionization equation* and the *acid ionization expression* for any given acid.	○	○	○
	276	Write the *base ionization equation* and the *base ionization expression* for any given base.	○	○	○
	277	Find the K_a value of an acid in the K_a table.	○	○	○
	277 – 278	Relate the strength of an acid to the strength of its conjugate base and vice-versa.	○	○	○
	279	Describe and explain periodic trends in *binary acid* strength.	○	○	○
	280	Cite two factors that influence the strength of *ternary acids.*	○	○	○
	280	Cite two factors that influence the strength of *carboxylic acids.*	○	○	○
	282 - 283	Determine whether the forward or reverse reaction is favoured in any *Brønsted-Lowry acid-base equilibrium.*	○	○	○
	284	Describe the *levelling effect.*	○	○	○
5.3	289	Provide the chemical equation for the *autoionization* of water, the K_w expression and the value of K_w at room temp.	○	○	○
	290	Define *acidic, basic,* and *neutral* in terms of the relative concentrations of H^+ and OH^-.	○	○	○
	291	Calculate the $[H^+]$ and $[OH^-]$ in strong acid and strong base solutions.	○	○	○
	292	Calculate the $[H^+]$ and $[OH^-]$ that result from mixing particular amounts of a strong acid and a strong base.	○	○	○

Edvantage Science AP Chemistry 2

Chapter 5

Traffic Light Study Guide

Section	Page	I can ...	Red	Yellow	Green
5.4	296 - 297	Calculate a solution's *pH* from its $[H^+]$, taking care to express the pH to the appropriate number of sig.figs.	○	○	○
	297	Cite two ways to measure a solution's pH.	○	○	○
	298	Calculate a solution's $[H^+]$ from its pH, taking care to express the $[H^+]$ to the appropriate number of sig.figs.	○	○	○
	299 - 302	Interconvert $[H^+]$, $[OH^-]$, pH and pOH.	○	○	○
	300 - 301	Identify an aqueous solution at room temperature as being acidic, basic (alkaline), or neutral, from its pH or its pOH.	○	○	○
	304 - 305	Calculate the pH and pOH that result from mixing particular amounts of a strong acid and a strong base.	○	○	○
5.5	311 - 314	Calculate an acid solution's $[H^+]$ from the acid's K_a and the (initial) [acid].	○	○	○
	315 - 316	Calculate an acid solution's concentration from the acid's K_a and the solution's pH.	○	○	○
	316	Calculate an acid's K_a from the acid solution's concentration and its pH.	○	○	○
	318	Calculate the K_b of a base from the K_a of its conjugate acid and K_w.	○	○	○
	319 - 320	Calculate a base solution's $[OH^-]$ from the base's K_b and the (initial) [base].	○	○	○
	321 - 322	Calculate a base solution's concentration from the base's K_b and the solution's pH.	○	○	○
	323	Calculate a base's K_b from the base solution's concentration and its pH.	○	○	○

For more support in AP Chemistry 2, go to edvantagescience.com

5.1 Identifying Acids and Bases

1. How are the Arrhenius and Brønsted-Lowry definitions of an acid and base similar? How are they different? Use examples.

2. Explain why the H^+ ion is the same as a proton.

3. A hydronium ion is formed when water accepts a proton. Draw a Lewis structure for water, and explain why water will accept a proton. Draw the Lewis structure for a hydronium ion.

4. In the following equations, identify the acids and bases in the forward and reverse reactions. Identify the conjugate acid-base pairs.
   (a) $NH_3 + H_3PO_4 \rightleftharpoons NH_4^+ + H_2PO_4^-$

   (b) $H_2PO_4^- + SO_3^{2-} \rightleftharpoons HSO_3^- + HPO_4^{2-}$

   (c) $CH_3NH_2 + CH_3COOH \rightleftharpoons CH_3COO^- + CH_3NH_3^+$

5. Formic acid, HCOOH, is the substance responsible for the sting in ant bites. Write an equation showing it acting as an acid when reacted with water. Label the acids and bases in the forward and reverse reactions. Identify the two conjugate acid-base pairs.

6. Pyridine, C_5H_5N, is a Brønsted-Lowry base. It is used in the production of many pharmaceuticals. Write an equation showing it acting as a base when reacted with water. Label the acids and bases in the forward and reverse reactions. Identify the two conjugate acid-base pairs.

7. Sodium hypochlorite solution is also known as bleach. It contains the hypochlorite ion ClO^-.
   (a) Write an equation for the reaction between hypochlorite ion and ammonium ion. Label the acids and bases in the forward and reverse reactions. Identify the two conjugate acid-base pairs.

   (b) This equilibrium favors the reactants. Which of the acids is stronger and donates protons more readily?

8. (a) Explain how to write the formula for the conjugate acid of a given base. Use an example.

   (b) Explain how to write the formula for the conjugate base of a given acid. Use an example.

9. (a) Hydrogen peroxide, H_2O_2, is a Brønsted Lowry acid. It is used as an antiseptic and bleaching agent. Write the formula for the conjugate base of hydrogen peroxide.

   (b) Hydrazine, N_2H_4, is a Brønsted-Lowry base used as a rocket fuel. Write the formula for the conjugate acid of hydrazine.

   (c) Phenol, HOC_6H_5, is a Brønsted-Lowry acid used to make plastics, nylon, and slimicides. Write the formula for its conjugate base.

   (d) Aniline, $C_6H_5NH_2$, is a Brønsted-Lowry base used to make polyurethane. Write the formula for its conjugate acid.

10. Define the term *amphiprotic*. List four amphiprotic substances.

11. Baking soda contains sodium bicarbonate.
    (a) Write two equations demonstrating the amphiprotic nature of the bicarbonate ion with water. Describe a test you could perform to identify which equilibrium is more likely to occur.

    (b) Bicarbonate produces CO_2 gas in the batter of cookies or cakes, which makes the batter rise as it bakes. Which of the two equations in (a) represents the action of bicarbonate ion in baking?

12. Water is amphiprotic. Write a reaction showing a water molecule acting as an acid reacting with a water molecule acting as a base. Label the acids and bases for the forward and reverse reactions. Identify the conjugate acid-base pairs.

5.1 Activity: Conjugate Pairs Memory Game

Question

How many conjugate acid-base pairs can you identify?

Materials

- grid of conjugate pairs, cut into cards
- scissors

Procedure

1. Go to edvantagescience.com for a page of symbols and formulas.
2. Cut along the grid lines to make a set of cards. Each card will have one symbol or formula on it.
3. Place the cards face down on the table in a 6 × 6 grid.
4. Play in groups of two or three. The first player turns over two cards. If the two substances are a conjugate acid-base pair, the player keeps the two cards and gets one more turn. If they are not a conjugate acid-base pair, the player turns the cards face down again after everyone has seen them.
5. The next player turns over two cards, again looking for a conjugate pair.
6. The play continues until all conjugate acid-base pair cards are collected. The winner is the player with the most cards.

Results and Discussion

1. Define an acid-base conjugate pair.

2. Explain why H_2SO_3 and SO_3^{2-} are not a conjugate pair.

5.2 The Strengths of Acids and Bases

1. Classify the following as strong or weak acids or bases.
   (a) sodium oxide — used in glass making

   (b) boric acid — used to manufacture fiberglass, antiseptics, and insecticides

   (c) perchloric acid — used to make ammonium perchlorate for rocket fuel

   (d) phosphate ion — present in the cleaner TSP (trisodium phosphate)

2. For any of the substances above that are weak, write an equation showing how they react in water, then write its corresponding K_a or K_b expression.

3. A student tests the electrical conductivity of a 2.0 M oxalic acid solution and compares it to the conductivity of 2.0 M hydroiodic acid. Explain how the hydroiodic acid could have a greater conductivity than the oxalic acid.

4. Calculate the total ion concentration in a solution of 2.0 M nitric acid. Explain why you cannot use this method to calculate the concentration of ions in 2.0 M nitrous acid.

5. Give an example of a
   (a) concentrated weak base

   (b) dilute strong acid

6. (a) Rank the following 0.1 M solutions in order from least electrical conductivity to greatest electrical conductivity: carbonic acid, citric acid, sulfuric acid, sulfurous acid, and water.

(b) Rank the following bases in order from strongest to weakest: monohydrogen phosphate ion, carbonate ion, fluoride ion, ammonia, nitrite ion, and water.

7. Write the equation for the reaction of each of the following acids in water and its corresponding K_a expression:
(a) monohydrogen citrate ion

(b) dihydrogen citrate ion

(c) aluminum ion

(d) hydrogen peroxide

8. Write the equation for the reaction of each of the following bases in water and its corresponding K_b expression:
(a) ammonia

(b) benzoate ion

(c) acetate ion

(d) monohydrogen citrate ion

(e) pyradine (C_5H_5N).

9. For the following, complete the equilibria, then state whether reactants or products are favored.

(a)

$Fe(H_2O)_6^{3+}(aq) + HO_2^-(aq) \rightleftharpoons$

(b)

$H_2SO_3(aq) + IO_3^-(aq) \rightleftharpoons$

(c)

$CN^-(aq) + H_2PO_4^-(aq) \rightleftharpoons$

10. Using the substances H_2CO_3, HCO_3^-, $H_2C_2O_4$ and $HC_2O_4^-$, write an equilibrium equation with a $K_{eq} > 1$.

11. Consider the following equilibria:

$H_2SiO_3 + BrO^- \rightleftharpoons HBrO + HSiO_3^- \quad K_{eq} = 0.095$

$HClO + BrO^- \rightleftharpoons HBrO + ClO^- \quad K_{eq} = 14$

Rank the acids H_2SiO_3, HClO, and HBrO from strongest to weakest.

12. Explain why HCl, HBr, and HI are equally strong in water. Use balanced chemical equations in your answer.

5.2 Activity: Determining the Relative Strengths of Six Acids

Question

You are given six unknown weak acid solutions of the same concentration. The three weak acid indicators (HIn) are first mixed with HCl and NaOH. Can you build a table of relative acid strengths for six unknown solutions?

Procedure

1. Consider the following data collected when the indicated solutions are mixed:

	HIn_1/In_1^-	HIn_2/In_2^-	HIn_3/In_3^-
HCl	red	yellow	colorless
NaOH	yellow	red	purple
HA_1/A_1^-	red	yellow	purple
HA_2/A_2^-	red	yellow	colorless
HA_3/A_3^-	yellow	yellow	purple

2. There are six unknown weak acid solutions containing a conjugate acid-base pair. Three of the acids are HA_1, HA_2, and HA_3. The other three acids are chemical indicators HIn_1, HIn_2, and HIn_3. A chemical indicator is a weak acid in which its conjugate acid has a different color than its conjugate base. In the indicator solution, both the acid form (HIn) and the base form (In^-) exist in equilibrium.
3. When indicator 1 (HIn_1) is mixed with HCl, the HCl will donate a H^+ ion because it is a strong acid. If HCl acts as an acid, then it will donate a H^+ ion to the base form of the indicator:
   $HCl + In_1^- \rightarrow HIn_1 + Cl^-$
   According to the data in step 1, indicator 1 turns red in HCl. Therefore, HIn must be red. Likewise, In^- must be yellow because the OH^- in NaOH accepts a H^+ ion from HIn to form In^-. We know then that HIn = red and In^- = yellow.
4. When we mix unknown acid 1 (HA_1) with indicator 1 (HIn_1) we see red. The equilibrium established may be written as:
   $HA_1 + In_1^- \rightleftharpoons HIn_1 + A_1^-$
   yellow red
   Knowing that HIn_1 is red, we conclude that products are favored in this equilibrium. Therefore, HA_1 is a stronger acid than HIn_1.
5. Fill in the table below by comparing the strength of each pair of acids HA to HIn. The first one has been filled in for you from the discussion above.

	HIn_1/In_1^-	HIn_2/In_2^-	HIn_3/In_3^-
HA_1/A_1^-	$HA_1 > HIn_1$		
HA_2/A_2^-			
HA_3/A_3^-			

Results and Discussion

1. Rank the six unknown acids in order from strongest to weakest:
   _________ > _________ > _________ > _________ > _________ > _________
2. Construct a table similar to Table 5.2.1 Relative Strengths of Brønsted-Lowry Acids and Bases using the six unknown acids. Be sure to include ionization equations and arrows on each side of the table labelled: "Increasing strength of acid" and "Increasing strength of base."

5.3 The Ionization of Water

1. In its pure liquid form, ammonia (NH_3) undergoes autoionization. Write an equation to show how ammonia autoionizes.

2. Complete the following table:

$[H_3O^+]$	$[OH^-]$	Acidic, Basic, or Neutral?
	6.0 M	
3.2×10^{-4} M		
	9.2×10^{-12} M	
2.5 M		
	4.7×10^{-5} M	

3. The autoionization of water has $\Delta H = 57.1$ kJ/mol. Write the equation for the autoionization of water including the energy term. Explain how the value of K_w changes with temperature.

4. The K_w for water at 1°C is 1.0×10^{-15}. Calculate the $[H_3O^+]$ and $[OH^-]$ in 0.20 M HI at this temperature.

5. Human urine has a $[H_3O^+] = 6.3 \times 10^{-7}$ M. What is the $[OH^-]$, and is urine acidic, basic, or neutral?

6. Complete the table:

Temperature	K_w	$[H_3O^+]$	$[OH^-]$	Acidic, Basic, or Neutral?
50° C	5.5×10^{-14}			
100° C	5.1×10^{-13}			

7. Heavy water (D_2O) is used in CANDU reactors as a moderator. In heavy water, the hydrogen atoms are H-2 called *deuterium* and symbolized as D. In a sample of heavy water at 50°C, $[OD^-] = 8.9 \times 10^{-8}$ M. Calculate K_w for heavy water.

8. Calculate the $[H_3O^+]$ and $[OH^-]$ in a saturated solution of calcium hydroxide. ($K_{sp} = 4.7 \times 10^{-6}$)

9. A student combines the following solutions:
Calculate the $[H_3O^+]$ and $[OH^-]$ in the resulting solution.

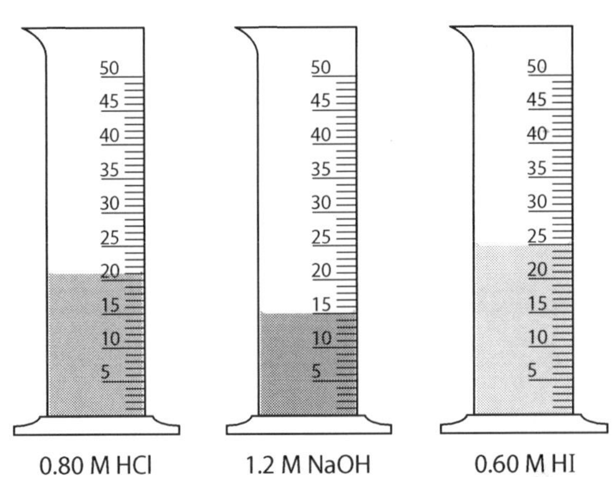

10. What mass of strontium hydroxide must be added to 150. mL of 0.250 M nitric acid to produce a solution with $[OH^-] = 0.010$ M?

5.3 Activity: Counting Water Molecules and Hydronium Ions

Question

How many water molecules does it take to produce one hydronium ion?

Procedure

1. Calculate the number of water molecules present in 1.0 L of water using the density of water (1.00 g/mL) and its molar mass.
2. Calculate the number of hydronium ions in 1.0 L of water. (Hint: You need the $[H_3O^+]$ in pure water from step 1.)
3. Using the above answers, calculate the ratio of ions/molecules. This is the percentage ionization of water.
4. Using the ratio above, calculate the number of water molecules required to produce one hydronium ion.

Results and Discussion

1. From the ratio of ions to molecules, it is evident that an extremely small percentage of water molecules actually ionize. Because there are an enormously large number of molecules present in the solutions we use, a reasonable number of hydronium and hydroxide ions are present. What volume of water contains only one hydronium ion?

5.4 pH and pOH

(Assume all solutions are at 25°C unless otherwise indicated.)

1. Define pH and pOH using a statement and an equation for each.

2. Why do we use Sorensen's pH and pOH scales to express hydronium and hydroxide concentrations in aqueous solutions?

3. Complete the following table, expressing each value to the proper number of significant figures.

$[H_3O^+]$	pH	Acidic/Basic/Neutral
3.50×10^{-6} M		
	11.51	
0.00550 M		
	0.00	
6.8×10^{-9} M		

4. Complete the following table, expressing each value to the proper number of significant figures.

$[OH^-]$	pOH	Acidic/Basic/Neutral
7.2×10^{-9} M		
	9.55	
4.88×10^{-4} M		
	14.00	
0.000625 M		

5. Complete the following statements:
   (a) As a solution's pOH value and $[H_3O^+]$ both decrease, the solution becomes more ______________ (acidic or basic).

   (b) As a solution's pH value and $[OH^-]$ both decrease, the solution becomes more ______________ (acidic or basic)

   (c) The ________________ (sum or product) of the $[H_3O^+]$ and $[OH^-]$ equals K_w.

   (d) The ________________ (sum or product) of pH and pOH equals pK_w.

6. Complete the following table, expressing each value to the proper number of significant figures.

$[H_3O^+]$	pOH	Acidic/Basic/Neutral
0.0342 M		
	8.400	
7.2×10^{-12} M		
	3.215	

7. For pure water at 60.0°C, the value of $pK_w = 13.02$. Calculate the pH at this temperature and decide if the water is acidic, basic, or neutral.

8. Calculate the pH of a 0.30 M solution of $Sr(OH)_2$.

9. A 2.00 g sample of pure NaOH is dissolved in water to produce 500.0 mL of solution. Calculate the pH of this solution.

10. A sample of HI is dissolved in water to make 2.0 L of solution. The pH of this solution is found to be 2.50. Calculate the mass of HI dissolved in this solution.

11. Complete the following table, expressing each value to the proper number of significant figures.

$[H_3O^+]$	$[OH^-]$	pOH	pH	Acidic/Basic/Neutral
5.620×10^{-5} M				
	0.000450 M			
		12.50		
			10.5	

12. Calculate the pH resulting from mixing 75.0 mL of 0.50 M HNO_3 with 125.0 mL of a solution containing 0.20 g NaOH.

13. Calculate the pH of the solution that results from mixing 200.0 mL of a solution with a pH of 1.50 with 300.0 mL of a solution having a pOH of 1.50.

14. Calculate the pH of a solution that is produced when 3.2 g of HI is added to 500.0 mL of a solution having a pH of 13.00. Assume no volume change.

15. The following three solutions are mixed together:
    25.0 mL of 0.20 M HCl + 35.0 mL of 0.15 M HNO_3 + 40.0 mL of 0.30 M NaOH
    Calculate the pH of the final solution.

16. What mass of HCl should be added to 450.0 mL of 0.0350 M KOH to produce a solution with a pH of 11.750? (Assume no volume change.)

17. What mass of LiOH must be added to 500.0 mL of 0.0125 M HCl to produce a solution with a pH of 2.75? (Assume no volume change.)

5.4 Activity: Finding Acidic and Basic Common Solutions

Question

Can you identify a series of common solutions as being acidic, basic, or neutral?

Background

Many common aqueous solutions used around your house are either acidic or basic. Some have pH values that are high or low enough to qualify them as being as hazardous as many chemicals used in the laboratory.

Procedure

1. For each of the common solutions listed below, only one of the four values has been provided. Determine the other three for each solution. (Assume all solutions are at 25°C.)
2. Classify each solution as either acidic, basic, or neutral.

Solution	pH	pOH	$[H_3O^+]$ M	$[OH^-]$ M	Acidic/Basic/Neutral
Unpolluted rainwater	5.5				
Saliva		7.3			
Stomach acid			0.031		
Tears				2.5×10^{-7}	
Vinegar	2.9				
Milk		7.6			
Milk of magnesia			3.2×10^{-11}		
Lemon juice				2.0×10^{-12}	
Tomato juice	4.2				
Orange juice		10.5			
Grapefruit juice			0.0010		
Liquid drain cleaner				1.0	
Black coffee	5.1				
Urine		8.0			
Blood			4.0×10^{-8}		
Laundry bleach				0.010	
Windex	10.7				
Pepto-Bismol		8.2			
Household ammonia			1.3×10^{-12}		
Red wine				3.2×10^{-12}	

Results and Discussion

1. Once you have completed the table, consider the last column. Are many of the solutions listed (or others that you found) actually neutral? Explain.

2. Do the majority of the solutions used for cleaning purposes have a low or a high pH? Try to find them in your home and see how many have a hazardous warning on their label.

3. Are the solutions that you consume generally acidic or basic?

5.5 Calculations Involving K_a and K_b

1. Calculate the $[H_3O^+]$, $[OH^-]$, pH, and pOH that results when 23.0 g of HCOOH is dissolved in enough water to produce 500.0 mL of solution.

2. At standard temperature and pressure, 5.6 L of H_2S is dissolved in enough water to produce 2.50 L of solution. Calculate the pH of this solution and percent ionization of H_2S.

3. The percent ionization of 0.100 M solution of an unknown acid is 1.34%. Calculate the pH of this solution and identify the acid.

4. Because of its high reactivity with glass, hydrofluoric acid is used to etch glass. What mass of HF would be required be required to produce 1.5 L of an aqueous solution with a pH of 2.00?

5. Phosphoric acid is used in rust removal and also to add a tangy sour taste to cola soft drinks. A solution of phosphoric acid is found to have a pOH of 12.50. Calculate the concentration of this acid.

6. Oxalic acid is a white crystalline solid. Some of its uses include rust removal, bleaching pulpwood, and even as an ingredient in baking powder. A 250.0 mL sample of an oxalic solution is found to have a pH of 2.35. What mass of oxalic acid would remain if this aqueous solution were evaporated to dryness?

7. Hypochlorous acid (HClO) is used mainly as an active sanitizer in water treatment. A 0.020 M solution of hypochlorous acid is found to have a pH of 4.62. Calculate the K_a for hypochlorous acid.

8. Phenylacetic acid ($C_6H_5CH_2COOH$) is used in some perfumes and in the production of some forms of penicillin. A 0.100 M solution of phenylacetic acid has a pOH of 11.34. Calculate the K_a of phenylacetic acid.

9. Complete the following table:

Conjugate Acid	Conjugate Base	K_a for Acid	pK_a	K_b for Base	pK_b
	NO_2^-				
H_2O_2					
	$C_6H_5O^-$				
HSO_4^-					

10. Complete the following table of amphiprotic ions:

Conjugate Acid	Conjugate Base	K_a for Acid	pK_a	K_b for Base	pK_b
	HPO_4^-				
$H_2C_6H_5O_7^-$					
	$H_2BO_3^-$				
HCO_3^-					

11. An aqueous solution is prepared by dissolving 5.6 L of NH_3 gas, measured at STP, in enough water to produce 750.0 mL of solution. Calculate the pH of this solution.

12. Isopropylamine, $(CH_3)_2CHNH_2$, is a weak base ($K_b = 4.7 \times 10^{-4}$) used in herbicides such as Roundup and some chemical weapons. Calculate the pOH and pH of a 0.60 M solution of isopropylamine.

13. What concentration of sulfite ions will produce a solution with a pH of 10.00?

14. Trimethylamine, $(CH_3)_3N$ is a weak base ($K_b = 6.3 \times 10^{-5}$). It is one of the compounds responsible for the smell of rotting fish and is used in a number of dyes. What volume of this gas, measured at STP, must be dissolved in 2.5 L of solution to give that solution a pOH of 2.50?

15. A 0.10 M solution of ethylamine, $C_2H_5NH_2$, is found to have a pOH of 2.14. Calculate the K_b for ethylamine.

5.5 Activity: An Organically Grown Table of Relative Acid Strengths

Question

Can you construct your own table of relative acid strengths using the relationships you have learned in this section to calculate the K_a values for a series of organic compounds?

Background

The vast majority of chemical compounds are organic (carbon-based) compounds and some of those are weak acids and bases. Given sufficient data, you can use various calculations to organize a collection of these compounds into a table from strongest to weakest acids similar to the Table of Relative Strengths of Brønsted-Lowry Acids and Bases (Table 5.2.1 and Table A5), which you have already seen.

Procedure

1. You will be given data relating to 15 organic compounds, 9 of which are weak acids, and 6 of which are weak bases. The data could include K_b, pK_b, pK_a, pH, and pOH information. None of the compounds appear on Table of Relative Strengths of Brønsted-Lowry Acids and Bases (Table 5.2.1 and Table A5). The data will not be presented in any particular order.
2. If given the acid, write the formula for the conjugate base and vice versa.
3. Use the data given to calculate the K_a value for each weak acid or for the conjugate acid of each weak base using any of the relationships discussed in this section. Before beginning, you may want to review the relationships below.
4. Place the equilibrium equation for each weak acid (or conjugate acid) reacting with water in order from strongest down to weakest acid as in an example provided.
5. Include in the right-hand section of the table you construct the K_a value you have calculated.
6. All of the acids are monoprotic carboxylic acids (containing –COOH) and so all of their conjugate bases will appear as $-COO^-$ following donation of the proton to water.
7. All of the weak bases are neutral amines containing nitrogen and so all of their conjugate acids will have an extra "H" on the nitrogen and a "+" charge following acceptance of a proton from the hydronium ion.
8. Consider the following when calculating the K_a values (Assume 25°C):
   - For conjugate acid-base pairs: $K_a \times K_b = K_w = 1.00 \times 10^{-14}$
   - For conjugate acid-base pairs: $pK_a + pK_b = pK_w = 14.00$
   - Review how to calculate K_a and K_b, given pH (or pOH) and $[HA]_{initial}$ (or $[B]_{initial}$).
9. Fill in the missing items in the table below and use the data provided to calculate the K_a values for all the acids and conjugate acids of the bases given in the table.
10. Then arrange all of the acids and conjugate acids in the correct order in the table, including the appropriate equilibrium equation for the examples given. Note that "soln" stands for "solution."

Compound Name	Formula for Conjugate Acid	Formula for Conjugate Base	Calculate K_a for Acid or Conjugate Acid Given
Acids			
chloroacetic acid	$ClCH_2COOH$		$pK_a = 2.85$
phenylacetic acid	C_7H_7COOH		pH of 1.0 M soln = 2.155
propanoic acid	C_2H_5COOH		K_b for conjugate base = 7.7×10^{-10}
pyruvic acid	C_2H_3OCOOH		pK_b for conjugate base = 11.45
lactic acid	C_2H_5OCOOH		pOH of 0.10 M soln = 11.57
acetylsalicylic acid	$C_8H_7O_2COOH$		K_b for conjugate base = 2.8×10^{-11}
glycolic acid	CH_3OCOOH		$pK_a = 3.82$
glyoxylic acid	$CHOCOOH$		pK_b for conjugate base = 10.54
glyceric acid	$C_2H_5O_2COOH$		pH of 1.0 M soln = 1.77
Bases			
pyridine		C_5H_5N	$K_b = 1.7 \times 10^{-9}$
trimethylamine		$(CH_3)_3N$	pOH of 0.10 M soln = 2.60
piperidine		$C_5H_{10}NH$	$pK_b = 2.89$
tert-butylamine		$(CH_3)_3CNH_2$	pH of a 1.0 M soln = 12.34
ethanolamine		$C_2H_5ONH_2$	pK_a of conjugate acid = 9.50
n-propylamine		$C_3H_7NH_2$	$pK_b = 3.46$

Relative Strengths of Some Organic Acids and Bases

Strength of Acid	Equilibrium Reaction With Water: Acid + H_2O $\rightleftharpoons$ H_3O^+ + Base	K_a Value	Strength of Base
Stronger ↑	$\rightleftharpoons$		Weaker ↓
	$\rightleftharpoons$		
	$\rightleftharpoons$		
	$\rightleftharpoons$		
	$\rightleftharpoons$		
	$\rightleftharpoons$		
	$\rightleftharpoons$		
	$\rightleftharpoons$		
	$\rightleftharpoons$		
	$\rightleftharpoons$		
	$\rightleftharpoons$		
	$\rightleftharpoons$		
	$\rightleftharpoons$		
	$\rightleftharpoons$		
Weaker	$\rightleftharpoons$		Stronger

Sample:

	Acid	+	H_2O	$\rightleftharpoons$	H_3O^+	+	Base	K_a Value	
	HCOOH (given an acid)	+	H_2O	$\rightleftharpoons$	H_3O^+	+	$HCOO^-$	1.8×10^{-4}	
	NH_4^+	+	H_2O	$\rightleftharpoons$	H_3O^+	+	$\mathbf{NH_3}$ (given a base)	5.6×10^{-10}	

Results and Discussion

1. Are the K_a values for these monoprotic carboxylic acids significantly different from each other in their orders of magnitude?
____
2. Which acid is the strongest and which base is the strongest? ________________________________
3. Use the K_a vlaues you have calculated to expand the Table of Relative Strengths of Acids and Bases, if you want to include these organic compounds.

5. 5 Data Tables

Table 5.2.1 *Relative Strengths of Brønsted-Lowry Acids and Bases (In aqueoous solution at room temperature)*

Strength of Acid	Name of Acid	Acid		Base	K_a	Strength of Base
STRONG	Perchloric	$HClO_4$	$\rightarrow$	$H^+ + ClO_4^-$	very large	
	Hydriodic	HI	$\rightarrow$	$H^+ + I^-$	very large	
	Hydrobromic	HBr	$\rightarrow$	$H^+ + Br^-$	very large	
	Hydrochloric	HCl	$\rightarrow$	$H^+ + Cl^-$	very large	
	Nitric	HNO_3	$\rightarrow$	$H^+ + NO_3^-$	very large	
	Sulfuric	H_2SO_4	$\rightarrow$	$H^+ + HSO_4^-$	very large	
	Hydronium Ion	H_3O^+	$\rightleftarrows$	$H^+ + H_2O$	1.0	WEAK
	Iodic	HIO_3	$\rightleftarrows$	$H^+ + IO_3^-$	1.7×10^{-1}	
	Oxalic	$H_2C_2O_4$	$\rightleftarrows$	$H^+ + HC_2O_4^-$	5.9×10^{-2}	
	Sulfurous (SO_2 +H_2O)	H_2SO_3	$\rightleftarrows$	$H^+ + HSO_3^-$	1.5×10^{-2}	
	Hydrogen sulfate ion	HSO_4^-	$\rightleftarrows$	$H^+ + SO_4^{2-}$	1.2×10^{-2}	
	Phosphoric	H_3PO_4	$\rightleftarrows$	$H^+ + H_2PO_4^-$	7.5×10^{-3}	
	Hexaaquoiron ion, iron(III) ion	$Fe(H_2O)_6^{3+}$	$\rightleftarrows$	$H^+ + Fe(H_2O)_5(OH)^{2+}$	6.0×10^{-3}	
	Citric	$H_3C_6H_5O_7$	$\rightleftarrows$	$H^+ + H_2C_6H_5O_7^-$	7.1×10^{-4}	
	Nitrous	HNO_2	$\rightleftarrows$	$H^+ + NO_2^-$	4.6×10^{-4}	
	Hydrofluoric	HF	$\rightleftarrows$	$H^+ + F^-$	3.5×10^{-4}	
	Methanoic, formic	$HCOOH$	$\rightleftarrows$	$H^+ + HCOO^-$	1.8×10^{-4}	
	Hexaaquochromium ion, chromium(III) ion	$Cr(H_2O)_6^{3+}$	$\rightleftarrows$	$H^+ + Cr(H_2O)_5(OH)^{2+}$	1.5×10^{-4}	
	Benzoic	C_6H_5COOH	$\rightleftarrows$	$H^+ + C_6H_5COO^-$	6.5×10^{-5}	
	Hydrogen oxalate ion	$HC_2O_4^-$	$\rightleftarrows$	$H^+ + C_2O_4^{2-}$	6.4×10^{-5}	
	Ethanoic, acetic	CH_3COOH	$\rightleftarrows$	$H^+ + CH_3COO^-$	1.8×10^{-5}	
	Dihydrogen citrate ion	$H_2C_6H_5O_7^-$	$\rightleftarrows$	$H^+ + HC_6H_5O_7^{2-}$	1.7×10^{-5}	
	Hexaaquoaluminum ion, aluminum ion	$Al(H_2O)_6^{3+}$	$\rightleftarrows$	$H^+ + Al(H_2O)_5(OH)^{2+}$	1.4×10^{-5}	
	Carbonic (CO_2 +H_2O)	H_2CO_3	$\rightleftarrows$	$H^+ + HCO_3^-$	4.3×10^{-7}	
	Monohydrogen citrate ion	$HC_6H_5O_7^{2-}$	$\rightleftarrows$	$H^+ + C_6H_5O_7^{3-}$	4.1×10^{-7}	
	Hydrogen sulfite ion	HSO_3^-	$\rightleftarrows$	$H^+ + SO_3^{2-}$	1.0×10^{-7}	
	Hydrogen sulfide	H_2S	$\rightleftarrows$	$H^+ + HS^-$	9.1×10^{-8}	
	Dihydrogen phosphate ion	$H_2PO_4^-$	$\rightleftarrows$	$H^+ + HPO_4^{2-}$	6.2×10^{-8}	
	Boric	H_3BO_3	$\rightleftarrows$	$H^+ + H_2BO_3^-$	7.3×10^{-10}	
	Ammonium ion	NH_4^+	$\rightleftarrows$	$H^+ + NH_3$	5.6×10^{-10}	
	Hydrocyanic	HCN	$\rightleftarrows$	$H^+ + CN^-$	4.9×10^{-10}	
	Phenol	C_6H_5OH	$\rightleftarrows$	$H^+ + C_6H_5O^-$	1.3×10^{-10}	
	Hydrogen carbonate ion	HCO_3^-	$\rightleftarrows$	$H^+ + CO_3^{2-}$	5.6×10^{-11}	
	Hydrogen peroxide	H_2O_2	$\rightleftarrows$	$H^+ + HO_2^-$	2.4×10^{-12}	
	Monohydrogen phosphate ion	HPO_4^{2-}	$\rightleftarrows$	$H^+ + PO_4^{3-}$	2.2×10^{-13}	
WEAK	Water	H_2O	$\rightleftarrows$	$H^+ + OH^-$	1.0×10^{-14}	
	Hydroxide ion	OH^-	$\leftarrow$	$H^+ + O^{2-}$	very small	
	Ammonia	NH_3	$\leftarrow$	$H^+ + NH_2^-$	very small	STRONG

(Left arrow: STRENGTH OF ACID, increasing upward from WEAK to STRONG. Right arrow: STRENGTH OF BASE, increasing downward from WEAK to STRONG.)

6 Applications of Acid-Base Reactions

This chapter focuses on the following AP Big Ideas from the College Board:

- Big Idea 3: Changes in matter involve the rearrangement and/or reorganization of atoms and/or the transfer of electrons.
- Big Idea 6: Any bond or intermolecular attraction that can be formed can be broken. These two processes are in a dynamic competition, sensitive to initial conditions and external perturbations.

By the end of this chapter, you should be able to do the following:

- Demonstrate an ability to design, perform, and analyze a titration experiment involving the following:
  - primary standards
  - standardized solutions
  - titration curves
  - appropriate indicators
- Describe an indicator as an equilibrium system
- Perform and interpret calculations involving the pH in a solution and K_a for an indicator
- Describe the hydrolysis of ions in salt solutions
- Analyse the extent of hydrolysis in salt solutions
- Describe buffers as equilibrium systems
- Describe the preparation of buffer systems
- Predict what will happen when oxides dissolve in rain water

---

By the end of this chapter, you should know the meaning of these **key terms**:

- acid rain
- buffers
- dissociation
- equation
- equivalence point (stoichiometric point)
- hydrolysis
- hydrolysis reaction
- indicator
- primary standards
- salt
- titration
- titration curve
- transition point

The freshwater African chichlid requires water having a pH between 8.0 and 9.2 to survive. The South American chichlid requires water with a pH between 6.4 and 7.0.

Chapter 6

Traffic Light Study Guide

Section	Page	I can …	Red	Yellow	Green
6.1	332	Define *hydrolysis*.	○	○	○
	333 - 342	Identify any given salt as neutral, acidic, or basic.	○	○	○
	333 - 335	Identify the ion and provide the hydrolysis reaction responsible for the acidity or alkalinity of any salt.	○	○	○
	334	Calculate the pH of a basic salt solution.	○	○	○
	336	Calculate the pH of an acidic salt solution.	○	○	○
	339 – 340	Determine whether an *amphoteric salt*, in particular, is acidic or basic. A compound that is *amphoteric* contains or consists of two independent species, one that is an acid and one that is a base.	○	○	○
	341 - 342	Determine whether an *amphiprotic ion* is acidic or basic.	○	○	○
6.2	348	Define a *buffer*.	○	○	○
	349 – 350	Describe the composition of a buffer.	○	○	○
	350 – 352	Describe and explain how an acidic buffer works.	○	○	○
	354 – 356	Describe and explain how a basic buffer works.	○	○	○
	357	(Extension) State the *Henderson-Hasselbalch equation*.	○	○	○
	357	Define *buffer capacity*. State and explain what it depends upon.	○	○	○
	357 – 358	Given the desired pH of a buffer, describe how to prepare it.	○	○	○
	359 - 360	Write the chemical equation for the *hemoglobin/oxyhemoglobin* equilibrium present in our blood and explain why a steady pH is critical to this equilibrium.	○	○	○
	360	Write the chemical equation for one buffer system that helps keep our blood pH relatively constant.	○	○	○
6.3	368	Supply 3 criteria that a reaction must satisfy to be used for a *titration*.	○	○	○
	368	Define the *equivalence point* of an acid-base titration.	○	○	○
	369 – 372	Describe an acid-base titration using the terms, *burette, pipette, flask, titrant, standard solution, analyte, indicator,* and *transition point*.	○	○	○
	372 – 373	List 4 properties of a *primary standard*, state its purpose, and provide an example of an acidic and a basic primary standard.	○	○	○
	374 – 376	Use titration data to calculate concentration, volume, or molar mass.	○	○	○
	377 - 378	Use data from the titration of an impure acid or base to calculate the acid or base's percent purity.	○	○	○

Edvantage Science AP Chemistry 2

Chapter 6

Traffic Light Study Guide

Section	Page	I can …	Red	Yellow	Green
6.4	385 – 388	Describe how *acid-base indicators* work.	○	○	○
	388 – 389	Calculate an indicator's K_a and state how to choose a suitable indicator for a titration.	○	○	○
	388 – 389	Determine the colour of a mixture of indicators in a solution of given pH (and vice-versa).	○	○	○
	391 – 394	Calculate the key points of a strong acid – strong base titration (initial, ½ equiv. pt., equiv. pt., & excess titrant) and draw its curve.	○	○	○
	495 – 401	Calculate the key points of a weak acid – strong base titration (initial, ½ equiv. pt., equiv. pt., & excess titrant) and draw its curve.	○	○	○
	401	Describe and explain the differences between strong acid-strong base titration curves and weak acid-strong base titration curves.	○	○	○
	404 – 407	Calculate the key points of a weak base – strong acid titration (initial, ½ equiv. pt., equiv. pt., & excess titrant) and draw its curve.	○	○	○
	391, 395, 403	Write formula and ionic equations for neutralization reactions.	○	○	○
6.5	415 – 416	Describe the reactions of metal oxides with water. Identify a metal oxide as being a *basic anhydride*, an *acidic anhydride* or *amphoteric*.	○	○	○
	417 – 418	Describe the reactions of non-metal oxides with water. Describe the general periodic trend pertaining to non-metal oxides.	○	○	○
	419 - 423	Outline the causes and consequences of *acid rain*, citing at least two chemical reactions involved.	○	○	○

For more support in AP Chemistry 2, go to edvantagescience.com

6.1 Hydrolysis of Salts — The Reactions of Ions with Water

1. Three separate unmarked beakers on a lab bench each contain 200 mL samples of 1.0 M clear, colorless aqueous solutions. You are told that one beaker contains $Ca(NO_3)_2$, one beaker contains K_3PO_4, and one beaker contains $Al(NO_3)_3$. Using the principles learned in this section, describe a simple test to identify the solutes in each solution.

2. Complete the following table for the six aqueous solutions by filling in the missing entries.

Salt Formula	Ion(s) that Hydrolyze(s)	Result for Aqueous Solution (Acidic, Basic, or Neutral)	Equation(s) for Hydrolysis Reaction(s) (if any)
$(NH_4)_2SO_3$			
$Al(IO_3)_3$			
RbF			
SrI_2			
KHC_2O_4			
$Fe_2(SO_4)_3$			

3. A 50.0 mL solution of 0.50 M KOH is combined with an equal volume of 0.50 M CH_3COOH.

(a) Write the chemical equation for this neutralization reaction.

(b) What salt concentration exists in the reaction vessel following the reaction?

(c) Calculate the pH of this solution. Begin by writing the equation for the predominant equilibrium that exists in the solution.

4. A 25.2 g sample of Na_2SO_3 is dissolved in enough water to make 500.0 mL of solution. Calculate the pH of this solution.

5. Copper(II) chloride dihydrate is a beautiful blue-green crystalline solid. The K_a for the tetraaquocopper(II) ion is 1.0×10^{-8}. What mass of $CuCl_2 \cdot 2\,H_2O$ would be required to produce 250.0 mL of an aqueous solution with a pH of 5.00?

6. Sodium cyanide is mainly used to extract gold and other precious metals in mining. Cyanide salts are also among the most rapidly acting of all poisons. A 300.0 mL aqueous solution of sodium cyanide is found to have a pH of 9.50. What mass of NaCN exists in this solution?

7. One of the main uses for ammonium perchlorate is in the production of solid rocket propellants. Calculate the pH of the solution produced by dissolving 470 g of the salt in enough water to make 5.0 L of solution.

8. Without performing any calculations, arrange the following 0.1 M aqueous solutions in order of increasing pH.

RbI NH_4Br KCN Li_2CO_3 $NaHSO_4$ $Cr(NO_3)_3$ Na_3PO_4 $FeCl_3$

_______ < _______ < _______ < _______ < _______ < _______ < _______ < _______

9. (a) What mass of KNO_2 will remain when 350.0 mL of an aqueous solution with a pH of 8.50 is evaporated to dryness?

(b) How will you observe the pH change as the volume of the solution decreases? Why?

10. Calculate the pH of a 0.500 M aqueous solution of N_2H_5Cl. The K_b for $N_2H_4 = 1.7 \times 10^{-6}$.

6.1 Activity: Hydrolysis — A Rainbow of Possibilities

Question

Can you predict the color that a universal indicator solution will display when added to a series of 10 different 0.1 M aqueous salt solutions?

Background

A universal indicator solution is a mixture of several chemical indicators, each of which undergoes a different color change over a different pH range. When the indicators are mixed, their colors and color changes combine over the entire range of the pH scale to display a series of rainbow-like hues depending on the hydronium concentration of the particular solution as shown in the table below.

pH	1	2	3	4	5	6	7	8	9	10	11	12	13	14
Colour	RED		ORANGE		YELLOW		GREEN			BLUE		PURPLE-VIOLET		

Procedure

1. Calculate the pH of the following 0.1 M aqueous solutions to determine the color displayed by the universal indicator when added to that solution. (The pH values for the first two salts are provided for you.)
   (a) $NaHSO_4$ (pH ≤ 3)

   (b) K_3PO_4 (pH ≥ 11)

   (c) NH_4NO_3

   (d) $Na_2C_2O_4$

2. Write the formula for each salt underneath the appropriate pH value and color in the diagram below.

3. Determine if the following 0.1 M aqueous solutions are acidic, basic, or neutral by comparing the K_a value for the cation to the K_b value for the anion in each salt.
   (a) $(NH_4)_2CO_3$

(b) $Fe_2(SO_4)_3$

(c) $(NH_4)_2C_2O_4$

4. The three solutions above have the following three pH values: 3.8, 6.5, and 8.5. Match each solution above to one of the pH values and write the formula for that salt underneath the appropriate pH value and color in the diagram below.

5. Determine if the following 0.1 M aqueous solutions should be acidic, basic, or neutral by comparing the K_a value to the K_b value for the anion in each salt.
   (a) KH_2PO_4

   (b) $NaHSO_3$

   (c) $KHCO_3$

6. The three solutions above have the following three pH values: 5.5, 4.0, and 9.0. Match each solution above to one of the pH values and write the formula for that salt underneath the appropriate pH value and color in the diagram below.

pH	1	2	3	4	5	6	7	8	9	10	11	12	13	14
Colour	RED		ORANGE		YELLOW		GREEN			BLUE		PURPLE-VIOLET		

Formulas

Results and Discussion

1. If possible, ask your teacher if you can test the results of your calculations by preparing as many of the above solutions as possible. Add a few drops of universal indicator to each and/or measure the pH values with a pH meter.

6.2 The Chemistry of Buffers

1. What is the purpose of an acid-base buffer?

2. Why do you think that the components of a buffer solution are normally a conjugate acid-base pair rather than any combination of a weak acid and a weak base?

3. Explain why a solution of 0.10 M HNO_3 and 0.10 M $NaNO_3$ cannot function as a buffer solution.

4. Each of the following compound pairs exists at a concentration 0.50 M in their respective solutions. Circle the solutions that represent buffers:

Na_2CO_3/KOH $NaCl/HCl$ C_6H_5COOH/KC_6H_5COO HNO_3/KNO_2

N_2H_4/NH_3 $CH_3NH_3NO_3/CH_3NH_2$ $K_2SO_3/KHSO_3$ CH_3COOH/HI

$HBr/NaOH$ KIO_3/HIO_3 $NaHS/H_2S$ HF/LiF $H_2O_2/RbHO_2$

5. Consider a buffer solution containing 0.30 M HCN and 0.30 M NaCN.
   (a) Without performing any calculations, state the $[H_3O^+]$ in the solution.

   (b) Is this solution considered to be an acidic or a basic buffer? Why?

   (c) Write the net ionic equation for the reaction occurring when a small amount of HCl is added to the solution. What happens to the pH of the solution after the HCl is added?

   (d) Write the net ionic equation for the reaction occurring when a small amount of NaOH is added to the solution. What happens to the pH of the solution after the NaOH is added?

6. Complete the following table for a buffer solution containing equal concentrations of HA and A^- when a small amount of strong acid is added and when a small amount of strong base is added.

Stress Applied	Net Ionic Equation	How [HA]/[A^-] Changes	How pH Changes
H_3O^+ added			
OH^- added			

7. Without performing any calculations, consult the table of K_a values (Table A5) and arrange the following buffer solutions (by letter) in order from lowest [H_3O^+] to highest [H_3O^+]:
(a) 1.0 M H_2S/1.0 M NaHS
(b) 0.50 M HCN/0.50 M KCN
(c) 0.25 M $NaHC_2O_4$/0.25 M $Na_2C_2O_4$
(d) 2.0 M HCOOH/2.0 M LiHCOO

________ < ________ < ________ < ________

8. What is meant by the term *buffer capacity* and what does it depend upon? Which of the buffer solutions listed in question 7 above would have the highest capacity?

9. List the following four buffer solutions (by letter) in order from highest to lowest capacity.
(a) 0.010 M KNO_2/0.010 M HNO_2
(b) 0.10 M CH_3COOH/0.10 M $NaCH_3COO$
(c) 0.0010 M NH_3/0.0010 M NH_4Cl
(d) 1.0 M HF/1.0 M NaF

________ > ________ > ________ > ________

10. What is meant by the term *buffer range*? How is it related to the pK_a value for the weak acid component of a buffer solution?

11. Describe the effect of lowering the [CO_2] in blood on the pH of the blood.

12. Describe the effect of *alkalosis* on the ability of hemoglobin to transport oxygen.

13. Describe the effect of *acidosis* on the ability of hemoglobin to transport oxygen.

14. **Challenge:** Consider carefully the components of a buffer solution and decide if a buffer solution could be *prepared* from 1.0 L of 1.0 M HNO_2 and sufficient NaOH? If so, how?

15. Use the Henderson-Hasselbalch equation to calculate the pH of each of the buffers mentioned in question 9 above.

16. Use the Henderson-Hasselbalch equation to answer the following:
    (a) A student requires a solution buffered to pH = 10.00 to study the effects of detergent runoff into aquatic ecosystems. She has just prepared a 1.0 L solution of 0.20 M $NaHCO_3$. What mass of Na_2CO_3 must be added to this solution to complete the buffer preparation? Assume no volume change.

    (b) Calculate the pH of this buffer solution following the addition of 0.0010 mol HCl.

17. Calculate the pH of the following buffer solutions:
    (a) 75.0 mL of 0.200 mol/L CH_3COOH mixed with 75.0 mL of 0.300 mol/L $NaCH_3COO$

    (b) 300. mL of 0.100 mol/L NH_3 combined with 200. mL of 0.200 mol/L NH_4Cl

18. A buffer solution contains 0.400 mol/L of CH_3COOH and 0.400 mol/L of $NaCH_3COO$. What is the pH of the buffer under the following conditions?
    (a) Before any acid or base is added

    (b) After adding 0.050 mol of HCl to 1.00 L of the buffer. Assume the total volume remains constant.

    (c) After adding 0.050 mol of NaOH to 1.00 L of the buffer. Assume the total volume remains constant.

19. A solution contains 0.0375 mol of HCOOH and 0.0325 mol of NaHCOO in a total volume of 1.00 L. Determine the pH following the addition of 0.0100 mol of HCl with no significant change in volume.

20. What ratio of [NaF]/[HF] is required to produce a buffer with a pH of 4.25?

21. How many grams of NH_4Br must be added to 0.500 mol of NH_3 to produce 1.00 L of buffer with a pH of 9.05?

22. (a) What is the pH of 1.00 L of buffer containing 0.180 mol of CH_3COOH and 0.200 mol of $NaCH_3C$

(b) How many moles of HCl must be added to this buffer to change the pH to:

(i) 4.600

(ii) 0.900

(c) The purpose of a buffer is to maintain a relatively constant pH when strong acids or bases are added. What caused the large drop in pH in (b)(ii)?

6.2 Activity: Over-The-Counter Buffer Chemistry

Question

What kinds of buffers are used in over-the-counter medicines?

Background

Many common over-the-counter medicines employ chemical principles that you are learning about. One of the most common and effective pain relievers or "analgesics" is the weak acid acetylsalicylic acid (ASA), $C_8H_7O_2COOH$. This product is marketed under various brands but the best-known one is Aspirin by the Bayer Corporation. (*Note that anyone under the age of 18 should not use ASA as children may develop Reye's syndrome, a potentially fatal disease that may occur with ASA use in treating flu or chickenpox.*)

One form of the product contains a "buffering agent" because some people are sensitive to the acidity level of this medication. That same "buffering agent" is used in several antacid remedies to neutralize excess stomach acid (HCl).

Procedure

1. Consider the advertisement shown here and answer the questions below.
   (a) Identify the ion in the compound listed on the box that acts as the "acid neutralizer" and buffers the ASA.

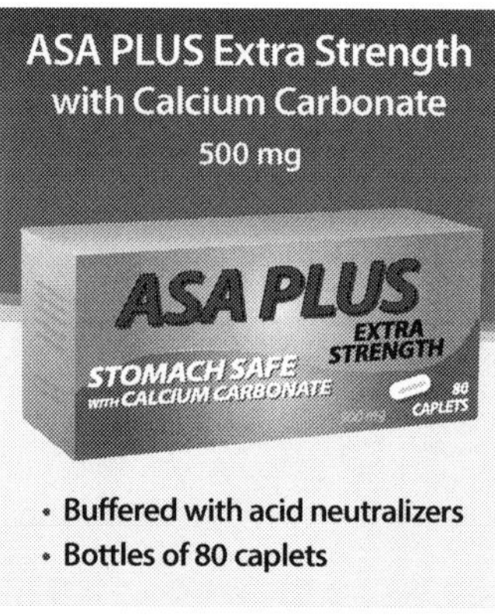

   (b) Write the net ionic equation corresponding to the reaction involving the "acid neutralizer" reacting with a small amount of strong acid.

   (c) Write the net ionic equation corresponding to the reaction occurring when a small amount of strong base is added to a relatively concentrated solution of ASA.

   (d) Consider the above net ionic equations and decide if a solution containing significant quantities of ASA and the ion identified as the acid neutralizer in question 1 would function well as a buffer solution? Why or why not?

2. Consider the antacid label shown here and note that the active ingredient is the same compound used to buffer the ASA above.

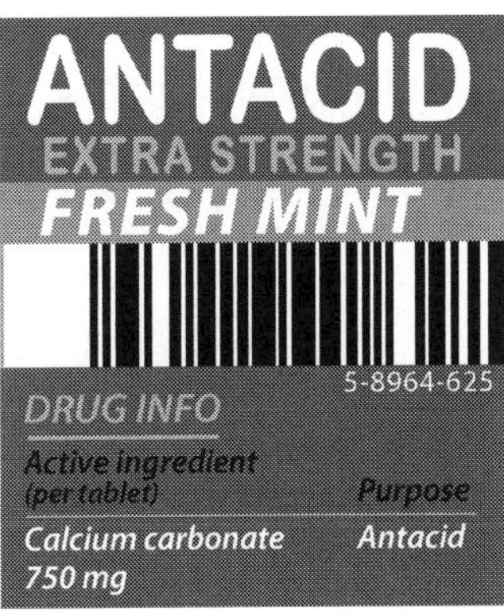

(a) Determine the pH of a buffer solution containing a 0.10 M solution of both the anion in the compound listed on the label and its conjugate acid.

(b) Would this solution be considered an acidic or a basic buffer?

3. Next time you're in a pharmacy, locate other antacid or "buffered" products on the shelves. Read the labels to determine if the active ingredient is the same or different than in the products listed here. If different, think about the chemistry associated with that ingredient and try to figure out how it works. (Thinking about the chemistry you encounter every day is *always* a good idea!)

6.3 Acid-Base Titrations — Analyzing with Volume

1. A student intends to titrate two 25.0 mL acidic solutions, each with a known concentration of approximately 0.1 M. One solution is hydrochloric acid and the other solution is acetic acid. He expects to require more of a standard NaOH solution to reach the equivalence point when titrating the HCl solution because it is a strong acid with a higher $[H_3O^+]$. Do you agree or disagree with the prediction? Explain your answer.

2. During a titration, a student adds water from a wash bottle to wash down some reactant solution that has splashed up in the Erlenmeyer flask. Although this changes the volume of the solution in the flask, she is confident that the accuracy of the titration will not be affected. Do you agree or disagree? Explain your answer.

3. A student must titrate a 25.0 mL sample of acetic acid solution whose concentration is known to be approximately 0.2 M. After adding a small amount of phenolphthalein indicator to the reaction flask, the student fills a 50 mL burette with a standardized 0.0650 M solution of NaOH and prepares to begin the titration. His lab partner insists that the titration cannot succeed. Do you agree or disagree with the lab partner? Explain your answer.

4. A student requires a standard solution of NaOH for a titration with a concentration as close as possible to 0.500 M. Using a digital balance, she carefully measures 20.00 g of NaOH. She quantitatively transfers it to a 1 L volumetric flask and adds the precise amount of water. She then calculates the concentration of the resulting solution to be 0.500 M and prepares to fill a burette and begin the titration. Her lab partner insists that the concentration is inaccurate. Do you agree or disagree with the lab partner? Would you expect the calculated concentration to be too high or too low? Explain your answer.

5. A student standardizing a solution of NaOH finds that 25.24 mL of that solution is required to neutralize a solution containing 0.835 g of KHP. Calculate the [NaOH].

6. A 21.56 mL solution of NaOH is standardized and found to have a concentration of 0.125 M. What mass of oxalic acid dihydrate would be required to standardize this solution?

7. A solution of NaOH is standardized and found to have a pH of 13.440. What volume of this solution must be added to 25.0 mL of a 0.156 M $H_2C_2O_4$ solution in a titration to neutralize the acid?

8. A 4.48 L sample of HCl gas, measured at STP, is dissolved in enough water to produce 400.0 mL of solution. A 25.0 mL sample of this solution is titrated with a 0.227 M $Sr(OH)_2$ solution. What volume of standard solution is required to reach the equivalence point?

9. A 0.665 g sample of an unknown monoprotic acid, HA, is dissolved in water and titrated with a standardized 0.2055 M KOH solution. If 26.51 mL of the basic solution is required to reach the equivalence point, calculate the molar mass of the acid.

10. A 5.47 g sample of an unknown diprotic acid is placed in a volumetric flask and then diluted to 250.0 mL. A 25.0 mL sample of this solution requires 23.6 mL of a 0.2231 M $Sr(OH)_2$ solution to completely neutralize the acid in a titration. Calculate the molar mass of the acid.

11. Tartaric acid, $C_4H_6O_6$, is a white crystalline diprotic organic acid. It occurs naturally in many plants, such as grapes and bananas, is often added to foods to give them a sour taste, and is one of the main acids found in wine. A 7.36 g sample of impure tartaric acid is diluted to 250.0 mL in a volumetric flask. A 25.0 mL portion of this solution is transferred to an Erlenmeyer flask and titrated against a 0.223 M standardized NaOH solution. If 40.31 mL of the basic solution is required to neutralize the acid, calculate the percent purity of the tartaric acid.

12. Sorbic acid, C_5H_7COOH, is a monoprotic organic acid that was first isolated from the berries of the mountain ash tree in 1859. It is a white crystalline solid used primarily as a food preservative. A 0.570 g sample of impure sorbic acid is dissolved in water to form 25.00 mL of solution. The acid solution requires 27.34 mL of 0.178 M KOH to reach the equivalence point. Calculate the percent purity of the sorbic acid.

13. Phenylacetic acid, C_7H_7COOH, is used in some perfumes and possesses a honey-like odor in low concentrations. A 0.992 g sample of impure phenylacetic acid dissolved in solution is titrated against a 0.105 M standard $Sr(OH)_2$ solution. If 31.07 mL of the standard solution is required to reach the equivalence point, calculate the percent purity of the acid.

14. Why is a titration considered to be a "volumetric" analysis?

6.3 Activity: Titration Experimental Design

Question

Can you identify the equipment and procedures associated with a typical titration and then employ them in designing a titration?

Background

As you have learned in this section, a titration is one of the most valuable analytical procedures employed by chemists. This activity is intended to review the equipment and reagents involved in a titration and then present you with the task of designing such an investigation.

Procedure

1. What is the function of each the following in a titration?
   (a) burette

   (b) volumetric pipette

   (c) Erlenmeyer flask

   (d) indicator

   (e) standard solution

   (f) acidic or basic primary standard

2. Why must every titration be repeated?

3. The concentration of a solution of acetylsalicylic acid, $C_8H_7O_2COOH$, must be determined very accurately for a clinical trial. The equipment and chemical reagents available to you to accomplish this are listed below. Using all of them, describe in point form and in order the laboratory procedures you would use.

Equipment	Reagents
• analytical balance • 100 mL beaker • 2 funnels • wash bottle • 250 mL volumetric flask • two 125 mL Erlenmeyer flasks • 50 mL burette • two 25 mL pipettes with suction bulbs • ring stand • burette clamp • safety goggles • lab apron	• pure oxalic acid dihydrate crystals • NaOH solution (approximately 0.1 M) • ASA solution (approximately 0.1 M) • phenolphthalein indicator solution

Titration Procedure

Results and Discussion

1. Write the balanced equation for the reaction that occurs during standardization of the basic solution and for the titration of the ASA solution.

2. (a) What salt solution exists at the equivalence point of the ASA titration?

   (b) Would you expect the pH of the solution at the equivalence point to be 7? Why or why not?

3. What concentration might be appropriate for the oxalic acid solution that you prepare?

4. Identify at least three possible sources of error and their impact on the experimental results.

6.4 A Closer Look at Titrations

1. Consider the following for a hypothetical indicator: $K_a = \frac{[H_3O^+][In^-]}{[HIn]} = 1.0 \times 10^{-7}$

   So, given that $\frac{K_a}{[H_3O^+]} = \frac{[In^-]}{[HIn]}$

   Complete the following table for three different solutions given that HIn is *yellow* and In^- is *blue*.

Solution	$[In^-]/[HIn]$ Ratio in Solution	Solution Color
0.0010 M HCl		
Pure water		
0.0010 M NaOH		

2. Equal concentrations of an indicator, HIn, and one of three different acids are placed in three separate flasks and the following data was obtained for each pair of compounds:

Solution →	0.1 M HNO_3	0.1 M HA1	0.1 M HA2
0.1 M HIn color	red	yellow	red

   Use the above data to list the three acids, HA1, HA2, and HIn, in order of increasing strength and explain your reasoning.

   ________ < ________ < ________

3. You are given four 0.10 M solutions without labels and told they are HCl, NaOH, $FeCl_3$, and NaCN. You are also told to choose only three indicators that will positively identify each solution. Complete the table below showing your choice of indicators and their colors in each solution.

Solution →	0.10 M HCl	0.10 M NaOH	0.10 M $FeCl_3$	0.10 M NaCN
Indicator 1:				
Indicator 2:				
Indicator 3:				

4. Complete the table below showing the reactants in three different titrations.
   (a) State if the pH at the equivalence point of each titration will be below, equal to, or above 7.
   (b) Select an appropriate indicator from the table of acid-base indicators (Table A6) for each titration. (There may be more than one correct choice for each titration.)

	HNO_3 + KOH	NaOH + HCOOH	HBr + NH_3
pH at equivalence pt.			
Indicator			

5. Bromcresol purple undergoes its color change from yellow to purple as pH increases from 5.2 through to 6.8.
   (a) Is bromcresol purple a stronger or a weaker acid than acetic acid? Explain your answer.

   (b) Would bromcresol purple be a good indicator to indicate that acetic acid is acidic? Why or why not?

6. The following 0.10 M solutions have had their labels removed: NaCl, K_3PO_4, LiHCOO, CH_3COOH, and HIO_3. The solutions are tested with three indicators and the results in the table below were observed.

	Bromthymol Blue	Methyl Orange	Thymolphthalein
Solution A	yellow	red	colorless
Solution B	green	yellow	colorless
Solution C	blue	yellow	blue
Solution D	yellow	yellow	colorless
Solution E	blue	yellow	colorless

Identify each solution:

A __________ B__________ C__________ D__________ E__________

7. Complete the following table:

Indicator	pK_a	K_a	Color in Pure Water	Color Displayed in 0.010 M NaOH	Color Displayed in 0.010 M HCl
Phenol red					
Methyl orange					
Alizarin yellow					

8. Complete each of the following statements relating to weak–strong titrations by placing the words "lower" or "higher" in each of the blank spaces in each statement.
   (a) In a weak acid–strong base titration, the weaker the acid being titrated, the __________ (lower or higher) the initial pH of the solution will be, and the __________ (lower or higher) the pH at the equivalence point will be.
   (b) In a weak base–strong acid titration, the weaker the base being titrated, the __________ (lower or higher) the initial pH of the solution will be, and the __________ (lower or higher) the pH at the equivalence point will be.

9. The chemistry of buffers and the hydrolysis of salts must both be considered when calculating the pH at different stages during the final two types of titrations we have discussed in this section. For each type of titration below, explain why in the appropriate space in the table:

	Calculating pH Halfway to the Equivalence Point (Chemistry of Buffers)	Calculating pH at the Equivalence Point (Hydrolysis of Salts)
Titration of a weak acid by a strong base		
Titration of a weak base by a strong acid		

10. Explain why the calculation of pH at the equivalence point for each of the titration types in question 8 above requires a *two-step* process.

11. A titration is performed in which a standard 0.200 M solution of NaOH is added to a 20.0 mL sample of a 0.250 M HCOOH solution.
    (a) Determine the pH halfway to the equivalence point.

    (b) Calculate the volume of standard solution required to reach the equivalence point.

    (c) Calculate the pH at the equivalence point.

12. A student titrates a solution of a weak monoprotic acid with a standardized NaOH solution. She monitors the pH with a pH meter and draws the titration curve. The curve reveals that, halfway to the equivalence point, the pH of the reaction mixture was 3.456. Identify the weak acid.

13. A solution of the weak base ethanolamine, $HOCH_2CH_2NH_2$, is titrated with a standard HCl solution. The pH is monitored with a pH meter and the titration curve is drawn. The curve reveals that, halfway to the equivalence point, the pH of the reaction mixture was 9.50. Calculate the K_b for ethanolamine.

14. The curve below shows the titration of a 0.10 M NaOH solution with a 0.10 M HCl solution. On the *same set of axes below*:
    (a) Sketch the titration curve for a 0.20 M NaOH solution being titrated with the same acid. Choose an appropriate indicator.

    (b) Sketch the titration curve for a 0.10 M NH_3 solution being titrated with the same acid. Choose an appropriate indicator.

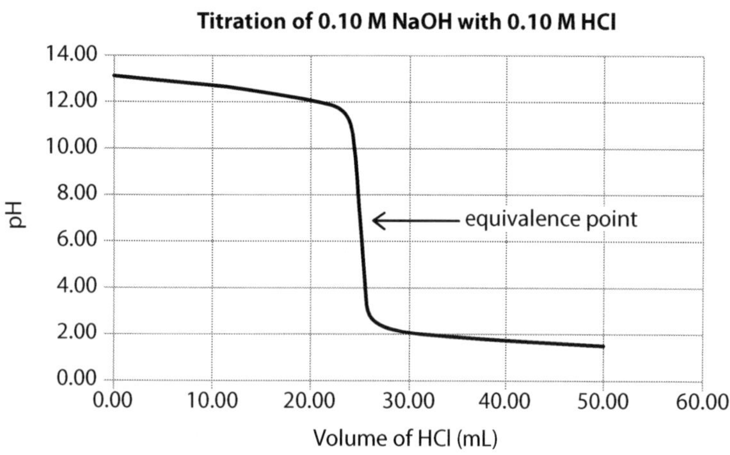

15. The curves we have discussed for the titration of both strong and weak acids have been limited to monoprotic acids. What do you think the titration curve might look like if the titration involved the titration of a weak *diprotic* acid with a strong base?

    (a) Sketch your suggested curve below:

    (b) What would you need to consider when selecting an indicator for such a titration?

6.4 Activity: A Titration Curve Summary

Question

How can you summarize the important aspects of each of the three types of titrations discussed in this section?

Background

As you have learned in this section, each type of titration we have considered has a different net ionic equation, a different titration curve with a characteristic shape and features, and a different equivalence point pH.

Procedure

1. Consider each of the titration types listed at the top of each column in the table on the next page. Complete each box in the table for each titration type using "HA" as the general formula for a typical weak acid and "B" as the general formula for a typical weak base.
2. Assume that the reacting solutions in each titration are at 0.100 M concentrations and that we begin with 25.0 mL aliquots in each reaction flask.
3. Although only a sketch of each curve is required, on each curve, clearly label the:
   - *x*- and *y*-axes
   - approximate pH at each equivalence point
   - volume of titrant required to reach the equivalence point
   - buffer region (if applicable)
4. In the boxes beneath each curve, state the reason that the equivalence pH is below, equal to, or above 7. Include any relevant chemical equation if applicable.
5. Use the completed table for review before your quizzes or tests.

A Titration Curve Summary Table

Strong Acid + Strong Base	Weak Acid + Strong Base	Weak Base + Strong Acid
Net Ionic Equation	**Net Ionic Equation**	**Net Ionic Equation**
Sketch of Titration Curve	**Sketch of Titration Curve**	**Sketch of Titration Curve**
Reason for Equivalence Point pH Value	**Reason for Equivalence Point pH Value**	**Reason for Equivalence Point pH Value**
Hydrolysis Reaction (if any)	**Hydrolysis Reaction (if any)**	**Hydrolysis Reaction (if any)**

Results and Discussion

1. The volume of titrant required to reach the equivalence point in each titration should be exactly the same. Explain why.

2. Explain how each of the two "weak–strong" titration curves can be used to determine one of either a K_a or a K_b value.

6.5 Non-metal and Metal Oxides in Water

1. Complete the following formula equations:

(a)	$Rb_2O(s)$	+	$H_2O(l)$	→
(b)	$SrO(s)$	+	$H_2O(l)$	→
(c)	$SeO_2(s)$	+	$H_2O(l)$	→
(d)	$N_2O_5(g)$	+	$H_2O(l)$	→

2. Calcium oxide (lime) is often added to lawns to *sweeten* the soil and help reduce moss growth. Write the chemical equation for the reaction that occurs in moist soil and indicate what is meant by the term *sweeten*.

3. Tetraphosphorus decaoxide, P_4O_{10}, is a potent dehydrating agent. This acidic anhydride is a white solid that reacts vigorously with water to produce a molecular acid that is listed on the Table of Relative Strengths of Brønsted-Lowry Acids and Bases (Table A5). Write the balanced equation for this reaction below.

4. Even though nitrogen and oxygen account for more than 99% of the gases in our atmosphere, they don't react to produce NO gas as they do when fossil fuels are burned in internal combustion engines. Why not?

5. In point-form below, identify four serious problems associated with acid precipitation.

6. Complete the following equations associated with the formation of acid rain:

(a) $SO_3(g)$ + $H_2O(l)$ →

(b) $NO_2(g)$ + $H_2O(l)$ →

7. Why can acid precipitation occur great distances from where the non-metal oxides causing the problem are actually produced?

8. Why are some lakes naturally protected from acid precipitation and what temporary protection can be employed to help those lakes that aren't?

9. (a) What is the purpose of "scrubbers" in coal-burning electrical power plants and smelters?

(b) What problems are associated with the process of scrubbing?

10. How does the catalytic converter in a vehicle's exhaust system help to reduce the problem of acid rain?

11. What role does ammonia play in the reduction of NO_x emissions from power plants?

6.5 Activity: The Canada–United States Air Quality Agreement Then and Now — Some Reasons for Optimism

Question

What can you learn from about efforts to reduce acid rain from the major international agreement between Canada and the United States relating to the control of acid rain?

Background

The *Canada-United States Air Quality Agreement* was signed by Canada and the United States in Ottawa, Ontario, on March 13, 1991, to address trans-boundary air pollution leading to acid rain.

Procedure

Part 1: The Original Document

1. Perform an Internet search using the title: "Canada-U.S. Air Quality Agreement."
2. When you locate the document, scroll down to "Section 1." Review the document carefully as you answer the following questions about sulfur dioxide and nitrogen oxide emissions for each country.
   (Note that 1 tonne = 1.1 tons)

Sulfur Dioxide

A. For the United States
   What was the target permanent national emissions cap for SO_2 produced by electrical utilities by the year 2010?

B. For Canada
   What was the target total permanent national emissions cap for SO_2 by the year 2000?

Nitrogen Oxides

A. For the United States
   Before the Acid Rain Program (ARP) was implemented, the projected annual NO_x emission levels from stationary sources for the year 2000 were 8.1 million tons. How far below this did the ARP set as a target level for total annual NO_x emissions for the year 2000? (Note that *stationary sources* refers to power plants, major combustion sources, and metal smelting operations, and *mobile sources* refers to all vehicles.)

B. For Canada
   Before the ARP was implemented, the projected annual NO_x emission levels from stationary sources for the year 2000 were 970 000 tonnes. How far below this did the ARP set as a target level for total annual NO_x emissions for the year 2000?

Part 2: The 2010 Progress Report

1. From the original page that loaded for the Air Quality Agreement, select the icon: "Canada-U.S. Air Quality Agreement Progress Report 2010."
2. Load the PDF file and select the "Acid Rain Annex." Review the document carefully as you answer the following questions.

Sulfur Dioxide Emission Reductions

A. For Canada

(a) In 2008, what were Canada's total SO_2 emissions and what percentage of the national cap established by the ARP do these represent?

(b) What continues to be the largest source of SO_2 emissions in Canada?

B. For the United States

(a) Consider the graph labeled "Figure 2. U.S. Emissions from Acid Rain Program Electric Generating Units, 1990–2009." In 2009, what were the total SO_2 emissions from the electric power sector and what percentage of the 2010 cap established by the ARP does this represent?

(b) Note that the ARP for the United States did *not* cover SO_2 emissions from non-electric power generators such as metal smelting. What were the *total* SO_2 emissions from all sources in the U.S. in 1980 and also in 2008? What percentage of that total do the emissions from the electric power sector represent?

Nitrogen Oxide Emission Reductions

A. For Canada

(a) In 2008, what were Canada's total NO_x emissions from stationary sources and what percentage of the original forecast for the year 2000 do they represent?

(b) What percentage of the total NO_x emissions do transportation sources represent?

B. For the United States

(a) In 2009, what were the total NO_x emissions from stationary sources (those covered by the ARP)?

(b) Before the Acid Rain Program (ARP) was implemented, the projected annual NO_x emission levels from stationary sources for the year 2000 were 8.1 million tons. What percentage of this projected amount does your answer to (a) represent?

Results and Discussion

The *Canada–United States Air Quality Agreement* is a large document with many clauses and statistics and many more questions (and discussions) are possible than the few we have mentioned here. Consider these questions to be merely the beginning of a much broader conversation concerning the problem of and potential solutions to acid rain. Your answers to the questions should convince you that there are reasons for optimism, but you should also note the final sentence of the "Overview" at the beginning of the 2010 Progress Report:

"However, despite these achievements, studies in each country indicate that although some damaged ecosystems are showing signs of recovery, further efforts are necessary to restore these ecosystems to their pre-acidified conditions."

Consider that restoration to be one of the challenges to you and your generation.

7 Oxidation-Reduction and Its Applications

This chapter focuses on the following AP Big Idea from the College Board:

- Big Idea 3: Changes in matter involve the rearrangement and/or reorganization of atoms and/or the transfer of electrons.

By the end of this chapter, you should be able to do the following:

- Describe oxidation and reduction processes
- Analyze the relative strengths of reducing and oxidizing agents
- Balance equations for redox reactions
- Determine the concentration of a species by performing a redox titration
- Analyze an electrochemical cell in terms of its components and their functions
- Describe how electrochemical concepts can be used in various practical applications
- Analyze the process of metal corrosion in electrochemical terms
- Analyze an electrolytic cell in terms of its components and their functions
- Describe how electrolytic concepts can be used in various practical applications

---

By the end of this chapter, you should know the meaning of these **key terms**:

- cathodic protection
- corrosion
- electrochemical cell
- electrode
- electrolysis
- electrolytic cell
- electroplating
- electrorefining
- Faraday's law
- half-cell
- half-reaction
- oxidation
- oxidation number
- oxidizing agent
- redox reaction
- redox titration
- reducing agent
- reduction
- volt

An old ship undergoing a redox reaction — rusting

Edvantage Science AP Chemistry 2

Chapter 7

Traffic Light Study Guide

Section	Page	I can …	Red	Yellow	Green
7.1	430	Define *oxidation-reduction/redox reactions* and cite types of reactions that are redox reactions.	○	○	○
	431 – 432	Determine the oxidation number of each atom in a chemical species.	○	○	○
	433 – 434	Define *oxidation* and *reduction* and relate each to an atom's change of oxidation number.	○	○	○
	434 - 436	Define *oxidizing agent* and *reducing agent* and identify each in a redox reaction.	○	○	○
7.2	441 - 442	Define *half-reaction*.	○	○	○
	442 – 443	Balance half-reactions both under acidic and basic conditions.	○	○	○
	445 – 446	Balance redox reactions using the half-reaction method.	○	○	○
	447 - 448	Balance *disproportionation* and *comproportionation* reactions.	○	○	○
7.3	457 - 460	Use the SRP Table to determine whether a spontaneous redox reaction, such as a single replacement reaction, will occur.	○	○	○
	460	Relate the strength of a reducing agent (e.g. A^-) to the strength of its complementary oxidizing agent (e.g. A).	○	○	○
	461	Define *oxidation potential* and *reduction potential* and read these off the SRP Table.	○	○	○
	462 - 463	Determine the predominant redox reaction that will occur in a mixture of oxidizing and reducing agents.	○	○	○
	464	Describe a redox titration and use redox titration data to calculate an analyte's concentration.	○	○	○
7.4	470 – 472	Draw a *standard electrochemical cell*, label its parts, and describe its operation.	○	○	○
	472	Describe a non-metal electrode.	○	○	○
	472 – 474	Use the SRP Table to predict *standard cell potentials* (E°).	○	○	○
	475 – 476	State the effect of altering half-cell concentrations on a given cell's potential.	○	○	○
	475 – 476	Describe and explain what happens to a cell's potential as it operates. State the meaning and voltage of a *cell at equilibrium*.	○	○	○
	476 - 479	Use the *Nernst Equation* to determine the potential of a cell with non-standard ion concentrations.	○	○	○

Edvantage Science AP Chemistry 2
Chapter 7
Traffic Light Study Guide

Section	Page	I can …	Red	Yellow	Green
7.4	476 - 479	Use the *Nernst Equation* to convert a cell's E° into K_{eq} (and vice-versa).	○	○	○
	480 - 482	Describe the basic structure of the alkaline dry cell, the lead-acid storage battery, and the fuel cell. Name the common uses for each.	○	○	○
	482 - 483	Define *corrosion*. Describe the chemistry of rusting. Cite factors that increase corrosion and describe methods (particularly *cathodic protection*) for protecting metals from corrosion.	○	○	○
7.5	492 – 493	Draw an *electrolytic cell*, label its parts, and describe its operation.	○	○	○
	493 – 494	Use the SRP Table to predict the voltage required to operate an electrolytic cell.	○	○	○
	495	Contrast the electrolytic cell with the electrochemical cell.	○	○	○
	495 – 497	Describe the difference between a *type 1*, a *type 2*, and a *type 3*, electrolytic cell.	○	○	○
	496 – 498	Use the SRP Table to determine the oxidation half-reaction and the reduction half-reaction that will occur in any given electrolytic cell.	○	○	○
	500 - 501	Describe the following applications of electrolysis: i. *electrowinning*, *electroplating*, and *electrorefining* ii. the *Héroult-Hall process* for producing aluminum iii. the *chloralkali industry* iv. *impressed current cathodic protection*	○	○	○
7.6	505 – 506	In an electrochemical or electrolytic cell, given *Faraday's constant (F)* and any two of the following, calculate the third. i. the amount of a chemical produced at an electrode ii. the amperage iii. the time the circuit was running.	○	○	○
	507 – 508	Calculate the Standard Free Energy Change (ΔG°) accompanying an electrochemical reaction.	○	○	○
	509 - 510	Interconvert the Standard Free Energy Change (ΔG°), the Standard Cell Potential (E°), and the Equilibrium Constant (K) for an electrochemical reaction and relate each to the reaction's spontaneity.	○	○	○

For more support in AP Chemistry 2, go to edvantagescience.com

7.1 Oxidation-Reduction

1. Elements that get oxidized (act as reducing agents) form (a)__________________ ions when they react. This means reducing agents are generally (b)__________________. Reducing agents may also be (c)________________ charged ions. The most active reducing agents likely belong to the (d)__________________ family on the periodic table. The most active oxidizing agents must belong to the (e)____________________ family.

2. Give the oxidation number for the underlined element in each of the following species:

   (a) $\underline{Ca}I_2$ (b) $\underline{O}F_2$ (c) $\underline{C}_6H_{12}O_6$ (d) $Rb_2\underline{O}_2$ (e) $\underline{S}_2O_3^{2-}$ (f) $Be\underline{H}_2$ (g) $\underline{Br}O^-$ (h) $\underline{Cl_2}$

3. (a) What is an oxidizing agent?

   (b) What is a reducing agent?

   (c) How would you expect electronegativity to be related to the strength of each?

4. For each of the following reactions, indicate the species being oxidized and reduced and show the oxidation numbers above their symbols.

   (a) $2\ KBrO_3(s) \rightarrow 2\ KBr(s) + 3\ O_2(g)$ Oxidized: Reduced:

   (b) $Sr(s) + 2\ CuNO_3(aq) \rightarrow Sr(NO_3)_2(aq) + 2\ Cu(s)$ Oxidized: Reduced:

   (c) $2\ F_2(g) + O_2(g) \rightarrow 2\ OF_2(g)$ Oxidized: Reduced:

   (d) $NH_4NO_3(s) \rightarrow N_2O(g) + 2\ H_2O(l)$ Oxidized: Reduced:

5. Determine the oxidizing and reducing agent in each of the following reactions. Then indicate the number of electrons transferred by one atom of the reducing agent.

(a) $2\,Sn(s) + O_2(g) \rightarrow 2\,SnO(s)$ OA: RA: No. e^-:

(b) $2\,V(s) + 5\,I_2(g) \rightarrow 2\,VI_5(s)$ OA: RA: No. e^-:

(c) $Sr(s) + 2\,HCl(aq) \rightarrow SrCl_2(aq) + H_2(g)$ OA: RA: No. e^-:

(d) $C_3H_8(g) + 5\,O_2(g) \rightarrow 3\,CO_2(g) + 4\,H_2O(g)$ OA: RA: No. e^-:

6. The pictures indicate the same reacting system following a 12 h period.

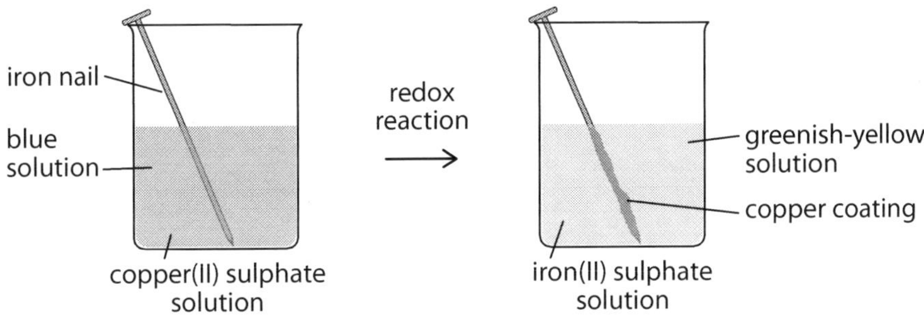

(a) Write a balanced redox equation (in net ionic form) to show what has occurred in the beaker over time.

(b) Which substance is the oxidizing agent? The reducing agent?

(c) How many electrons were transferred in the equation?

7. Give the oxidation number of the underlined element in each species:

(a) $\underline{P}^{3-}$ (b) $(NH_4)_2\underline{Zr}(SO_4)_3$ (c) $Na_2\underline{C}_2O_4$ (d) $\underline{N}_2H_5Cl$ (e) $\underline{Mn}O_4^{2-}$

8.

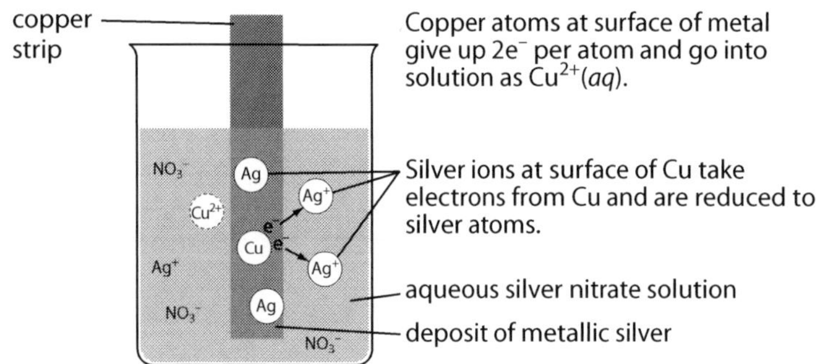

(a) Write a balanced net ionic equation to represent the redox reaction occurring in the beaker.

(b) Which substance is getting oxidized? Reduced?

(c) Which substance is the reducing agent? The oxidizing agent?

(d) How many electrons are transferred in each reaction?

9. What family on the periodic table would likely contain:

(a) The strongest reducing agents?

(b) The strongest oxidizing agents?

10. (a) Which of the following substances could be formed by the oxidation of ClO^-: ClO_4^-, Cl_2, ClO_2^-, Cl^-, ClO_3^-?

(b) The reduction of ClO^-?

7.1 Activity: Compare and Contrast Oxidizing and Reducing Agents

Question

How can you compare and contrast oxidizing and reducing agents?

Background

In previous activities you learned how useful it is to summarize the concepts you learn in "chunks" of material. You created a set of summary notes in the form of a table or chart of information. For this section, you will use the "compare and contrast" method to create a table as part of your summary notes for this section.

Procedure:

1. Use the outline provided below to organize what you've learned about oxidizing and reducing agents.
2. The first row has been completed as an example of what is expected. Note that there may be many other comparisons and contrasts (or similarities and differences) that you can add to your table. Don't feel limited to only those lines where clues have been provided.

Characteristic	Oxidizing Agent	Reducing Agent
Causes another species to be…	oxidized	reduced
Is itself ______ during reaction.		
Its oxidation number is__during reaction.		
Causes electrons to be...		
__________ electrons.		

Results and Discussion

You will find it very helpful to produce similar charts to help you summarize material for study. Add these to the dedicated section of your notebook for summary notes and refer to them from time to time to help you prepare for your unit and final examinations.

7.2 Balancing Oxidation-Reduction Equations

1. Electrons can be used to cancel positive charges or to increase negative charge. Complete the following table by indicating how many electrons must be added to the reactants or the products to balance the electrical charge.

	Reactants	Products	Add
e.g.	2+	3+	$1e^-$ to the products
(a)	3+	2–	
(b)	1–	3–	
(c)	2–	4+	
(d)	1+	5+	

Examine your answers. Are you following the suggestion to *always add electrons to the more positive side?*

2. Balance the electrical charge of each of the following half-reactions by adding the appropriate number of electrons to either the reactants or products. Indicate whether the half-reaction is an *oxidation* or a *reduction*.

(a) $2\,NO_3^- + 2\,H_2O \rightarrow N_2O_4 + 4\,OH^-$

(b) $2\,Cr^{3+} + 7\,H_2O \rightarrow Cr_2O_7^{2-} + 14\,H^+$

(c) $ClO_4^- + 4\,H_2O \rightarrow Cl^- + 8\,OH^-$

(d) $S_2O_5^{2-} + 3\,H_2O \rightarrow 2\,SO_4^{2-} + 6\,H^+$

3. Balance the following half-reactions under acidic conditions. Indicate whether each is an *oxidation* or a *reduction*.

(a) $ClO_4^- \rightarrow Cl_2$

(b) $FeO \rightarrow Fe_2O_3$

(c) $N_2O_4 \rightarrow NO_3^-$

4. Balance the following half-reactions under basic conditions. Indicate whether each is an *oxidation* or a *reduction*.

(a) $CrO_4^{2-} \rightarrow Cr(OH)_2$

(b) $S_2O_3^{2-} \rightarrow S_4O_6^{2-}$

(c) $IO_3^- + Cl^- \rightarrow ICl_2$

5. Balance the following reactions using the half-reaction method. Assume acidic conditions unless stated otherwise.

(a) $Sn^{2+} + MnO_4^- \rightarrow Sn^{4+} + MnO_2$ (basic)

(b) $V^{2+} + H_2SO_3 \rightarrow V^{3+} + S_2O_3^{2-}$

(c) $IO_3^- + I^- \rightarrow I_2$ (basic)

(d) $ClO_3^- + N_2H_4 \rightarrow NO + Cl^-$

(e) $NO_3^- + Zn \rightarrow Zn^{2+} + NO$ (basic)

(f) $ClO_3^- \rightarrow ClO_4^- + Cl^- + Cl_2$
Use the ΔON values to help you determine how to break this into two half-reactions.

(g) $SnS_3O_3 + MnO_4^- \rightarrow MnO_2 + SO_4^{2-} + Sn^{4+}$ (basic)

(h) $Mg_3(AsO_4)_2 + SiO_2 + C \rightarrow As_4 + MgSiO_3 + CO$

6. Balance the following using the ΔON method. Assume acidic conditions unless otherwise indicated.
   (a) $SeO_3^{2-} + F^- \rightarrow Se + F_2$

   (b) $ReO_4^- + Sb_2O_3 \rightarrow ReO_2 + Sb_2O_5$ (basic)

(c) $Pd + NO_3^- + I^- \rightarrow PdI_6^{2-} + NO$

(d) $Pb(OH)_4^{2-} + BrO^- \rightarrow PbO_2 + Br^-$ (basic)

7. Use the half-reaction method to balance the following reactions occurring in aqueous solution:

(a) $K_2Cr_2O_7 + CH_3CH_2OH + HCl \rightarrow CH_3COOH + KCl + CrCl_3 + H_2O$

You must first convert the equation into net ionic form, balance the net ionic equation, and then convert it back into the original formula equation. This is the reaction performed in the prototype BAT (Breath Alcohol Testing) mobiles.

(b) C.W. Scheele prepared chlorine gas in 1774 using the following reaction:

$NaCl + H_2SO_4 + MnO_2 \rightarrow Na_2SO_4 + MnCl_2 + H_2O + Cl_2$

7.2 Activity: A Balancing Short Cut (The Change in Oxidation Number Method)

Question

Is there a shorter way to balance redox reactions?

Background

The check we've been using for our half-reactions can be applied to full redox reactions to help determine the coefficients required to balance an equation without breaking it into halves. For many redox reactions, this can be fairly easy. In some cases, however, it can be extremely difficult.

Procedure

Study the examples shown below.

LEVEL I: $MnO_4^- + NO_2 \rightarrow NO_3^- + Mn^{2+}$

Level I problems do *not* require balancing of *"other" than O or H atoms.* There is only one species oxidized and one reduced.

Step 1: Assign oxidation numbers and identify the reduction and the oxidation number *changes*. We call these the ΔON values (change in oxidation number values).

+7------------------ ΔON = (–5)----------------2

+4 --- ΔON = (+1)-+5

$$MnO_4^- + NO_2 \rightarrow NO_3^- + Mn^{2+}$$

Step 2: Apply coefficients to make the increase in ΔON for the oxidation equal the decrease in ΔON for the reduction. This equalizes the electrons transferred.

$$MnO_4^- + 5\ NO_2 \rightarrow 5\ NO_3^- + Mn^{2+}$$

Step 3: Add the number of H_2O's needed to balance the oxygen atoms.

$$H_2O + MnO_4^- + 5\ NO_2 \rightarrow 5\ NO_3^- + Mn^{2+}$$

Step 4: Finish by adding H^+ ions to balance the hydrogen atoms.

$$H_2O + MnO_4^- + 5\ NO_2 \rightarrow 5\ NO_3^- + Mn^{2+} + 2\ H^+$$

Step 5: As always, perform a check at the end.

Species	Reactants	Products
Hydrogen	2	2
Manganese	1	1
Oxygen	15	15
Nitrogen	5	5
Charge	–1	–1

✔

LEVEL II: $P_4 \rightarrow HPO_4^{2-} + PH_3$ (basic)

This reaction is a disproportionation requiring the balance of an "other" atom to start.

Step 0: Begin by showing two P_4 molecules and placing coefficients to balance the P for each of the products as you would if you were using the half-reaction method.

$$P_4 + P_4 \rightarrow 4\ HPO_4^{2-} + 4\ PH_3$$

Step 1: Determine ΔON values. This becomes more difficult when there are "other" atoms to balance. As shown, each atom's oxidation number change must be accounted for.

0 -- ΔON = (+5 × 4 = <u>+20</u>) -- +5

0 ----------------ΔON = (–3 × 4 = <u>–12</u>) ---- –3

$$P_4 + P_4 \rightarrow 4\ HPO_4^{2-} + 4\ PH_3$$

Step 2: Equalize the electrons transferred by applying coefficients. In this case, the lowest common multiple of 20 and 12 is 60, thus the multipliers are 3 and 5 respectively.

$$3\ P_4 + 5\ P_4 \rightarrow 12\ HPO_4^{2-} + 20\ PH_3$$

Step 3: Add waters to balance oxygens.

$$48\ H_2O + 3\ P_4 + 5\ P_4 \rightarrow 12\ HPO_4^{2-} + 20\ PH_3$$

Step 4: Add hydrogen ions to balance hydrogens.

$$48\ H_2O + 3\ P_4 + 5\ P_4 \rightarrow 12\ HPO_4^{2-} + 20\ PH_3 + 24\ H^+$$

Basify: The addition of OH^- to both sides occurs at the very end only. In this case, you must reduce the coefficients to the lowest possible whole numbers.

$$48\ H_2O + 3\ P_4 + 5\ P_4 \rightarrow 12\ HPO_4^{2-} + 20\ PH_3 + 24\ H^+$$
$$24\ OH^- \qquad\qquad 24\ OH^-$$

$$(24\ OH^- + 24\ H_2O + 8\ P_4 \rightarrow 12\ HPO_4^{2-} + 20\ PH_3) \div 4$$

$$6\ OH^- + 6\ H_2O + 2\ P_4 \rightarrow 3\ HPO_4^{2-} + 5\ PH_3$$

Step 5: Check:

Species	Reactants	Products
Hydrogen	18	18
Phosphorus	8	8
Oxygen	12	12
Charge	−6	−6

It is always a good idea to add to your arsenal when it comes to problem-solving methods.
As practice makes perfect, try balancing these two reactions using the ΔON method. Check each.

1. $CN^- + ClO_3^- \rightarrow CNO^- + Cl_2$ (acidic)

2. $Fe + As_2O_3 \rightarrow AsH_3 + Fe^{3+}$ (basic)

Results and Discussion

1. Which method do you prefer when it comes to keeping your balance in the redox world? Explain why.

7.3 Using the Standard Reduction Potential (SRP) Table to Predict Redox Reactions

1. Will iodine spontaneously oxidize: (a) Fe^{2+}? (b) Sn?

2. Identify a metal ion that will spontaneously oxidize I^- but not Cl^-.

3. For each of the following, state whether a spontaneous reaction will occur and if so, write the balanced equation for the reaction.
   (a) $Mg + Al^{3+} \rightarrow$

   (b) $Cl^- + I_2 \rightarrow$

   (c) $Hg^{2+} + Ag \rightarrow$

4. Complete the following table:

Metals	Non-metals
bottom right of SRP table	
	tend to take electrons
give e^- to chemicals above them on the left	

5. For each of the following, state whether a spontaneous reaction will occur and if so, write the balanced net ionic equation for the reaction.
   (a) $Fe + Sn(NO_3)_2 \rightarrow$

   (b) $F_2 + KBr \rightarrow$

   (c) $Cu + NaI \rightarrow$

6. (a) Write the net ionic equation for the reaction between KI and $FeCl_3$.

   (b) Write the net ionic equation for the reaction between Br_2 and $FeCl_2$.

7. When tin(II) nitrate dissolves in acid the two dissociated ions react with each other. Write the net ionic equation for this reaction.

8. Would it be practical to store a 0.5 M $FeCl_3$ solution in an aluminum container? Explain.

9. State whether the forward or the reverse reaction is spontaneous.
   (a) $Sn^{4+} + 2\ Fe^{2+} \leftarrow\ ?\ \rightarrow 2\ Fe^{3+} + Sn^{2+}$

   (b) $Cr_2O_7^{2-} + 14\ H^+ + 3\ Cu \leftarrow\ ?\ \rightarrow 2\ Cr^{3+} + 7\ H_2O + 3\ Cu^{2+}$

10. One characteristic of acids is that they react with magnesium, liberating hydrogen gas. Write the balanced redox equation for this reaction.

11. Explain why silver oxidizes and then dissolves in 1 M nitric acid but not in 1 M hydrochloric acid.

12. A few drops of phenolphthalein are added to a petri dish of water. A small piece of sodium reacts violently when placed in the water, leaving pink tracks as it skips across the water's surface. The air ignites above the sodium producing a small flame. Write the redox reaction that occurs and briefly explain the pink tracks and the flame.

13. (a) Which has the greatest reduction potential, I_2, Ag^+, or Mg^{2+}?

    (b) Which has the greatest oxidation potential, I^-, Ag, or Mg?

14. The surface of a sheet of aluminum is observed to darken after being placed in a solution of gallium nitrate. From this observation, determine which has the greater reduction potential, Al^{3+} or Ga^{3+}.

15. (a) What is the reduction potential of $Br_2(l)$?

    (b) What is the oxidation potential of Zn(*s*)?

16. Write the predominant redox reaction that will occur in each of the following mixtures:
    (a) Co^{2+}, Cu, Mn^{2+}, and Fe

    (b) Cu, Hg, Cu^+, and Cr^{2+}

    (c) $CuCl_2(aq) + SnI_2(aq)$

17. If a zinc sheet were placed into a solution of $Cu^{2+}(aq)$ and $Fe^{3+}(aq)$ what would the predominant reaction be?

18. Each of the following redox reactions is spontaneous in the forward direction:

$A^{2+} + B \rightarrow B^{2+} + A$ $\quad$ $2\,C^{3+} + A \rightarrow 2\,C^{2+} + A^{2+}$ $\quad$ $B^{2+} + 2\,D \rightarrow 2\,D^{+} + B$

Which of the chemical species involved in these reactions is:

(a) the strongest oxidizing agent

(b) the strongest reducing agent

19. A chemist titrates 15.0 mL of KI(*aq*) to the equivalence point with 32.8 mL of 0.200 M $Na_2Cr_2O_7$. What is the [KI]?

$Cr_2O_7^{2-} + 14\,H^+ + 6\,I^- \rightarrow 2\,Cr^{3+} + 3\,I_2 + 7\,H_2O$

20. A $KMnO_4$ solution is standardized with oxalic acid. The equation for the redox reaction is:

$5\,H_2C_2O_4 + 2\,MnO_4^- + 6\,H^+ \rightarrow 10\,CO_2 + 2\,Mn^{2+} + 8\,H_2O$

What is the molar concentration of the $KMnO_4$ solution if 18.6 mL of the solution was required to titrate 0.105 g $H_2C_2O_4 \cdot 2H_2O$?

21. The legal limit for intoxication while driving has been a blood alcohol content (BAC) of 0.08% by mass for many years. Now the National Traffic Safety Board (NTSB) has called for reducing the limit to 0.05%. A 5.00 g sample of blood is titrated with 10.15 mL of 0.0150 M $K_2Cr_2O_7$. The dichromate ion acts as an oxidizing agent in the reaction of ethanol, C_2H_5OH, to form carbon dioxide and the Cr^{3+} ion.

(a) Balance the equation for the reaction that occurs during the titration.

(b) Calculate the percent alcohol by mass in the blood sample. Would this driver be considered legally impaired under the newly called for guidelines of a BAC of 0.05%?

7.3 Activity: Making an SRP Table

Question

How can you make a standard reduction potential table from a set of experimental data?

Background

Each redox reaction allows you to determine the relative position of its two half-reactions in the table. For example, from the following reaction in which L reduces M^{2+} you can infer that M^{2+} is a stronger oxidizing agent than L^+. M^+ is therefore above L^+ in the SRP table.

$L + M^{2+} \rightarrow 2\,L^+ + M$

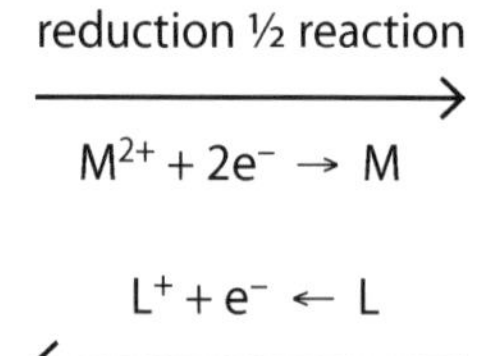

Procedure

Use the following information to produce an SRP table with six half-reactions.

1. $L + M^{2+} \rightarrow 2\,L^+ + M$
2. P^- reduces D^{3+} to D^{2+}.
3. Element Q is the strongest oxidizing agent. ($Q + e^- \rightarrow Q^-$)
4. $M + 2\,P \rightarrow M^{2+} + 2\,P^-$
5. L^+ oxidizes C to C^{2+}.

Results and Discussion

1. Fill in the SRP table below:

Oxidizing Agents		Reducing Agents
________________	⇌	________________
________________	⇌	________________
________________	⇌	________________
________________	⇌	________________
________________	⇌	________________
________________	⇌	________________

2. Which chemical species is the weakest reducing agent? ______________

3. Which chemical species has the lowest reduction potential? ___________

7.4 The Electrochemical Cell

1. Complete the following table for an electrochemical (metal electrode/metallic ions) cell.

Anode	Cathode
	reduction occurs
mass decreases	
	attracts cations
electrons flow away	

2. The electrochemical cell below consists of a strip of iron in 1.0 M $Fe(NO_3)_2$ and a strip of nickel in 1.0 M $Ni(NO_3)_2$. A salt bridge containing 1.0 M NH_4NO_3 connects these half-cells. A voltmeter connects the two electrodes. (Make sure your answers to the following questions refer specifically to the cell below. Generic responses that are true for any cell, such as "oxidation occurs at the anode," will not be marked correct.)

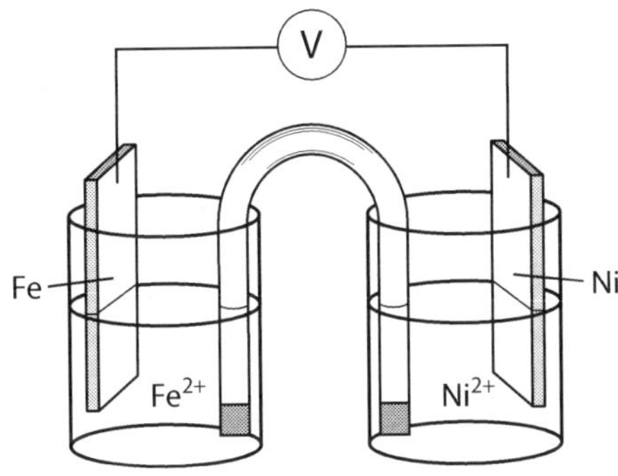

(a) Show the direction of electron flow on the diagram.
(b) In which half-cell does oxidation occur?

(c) Write the half-cell reactions involved.

(d) Label the anode and the cathode.
(e) What is the expected initial voltage?

(f) Describe the flow of the NH_4^+ and NO_3^- ions within the cell.

(g) Describe how the mass of each electrode changes as the cell operates.

3. Elemental bromine does not exist in nature. Bromine is a corrosive, red-brown liquid at room temperature. Draw and label a bromine half-cell.

Use the following diagram for questions 4 and 5.

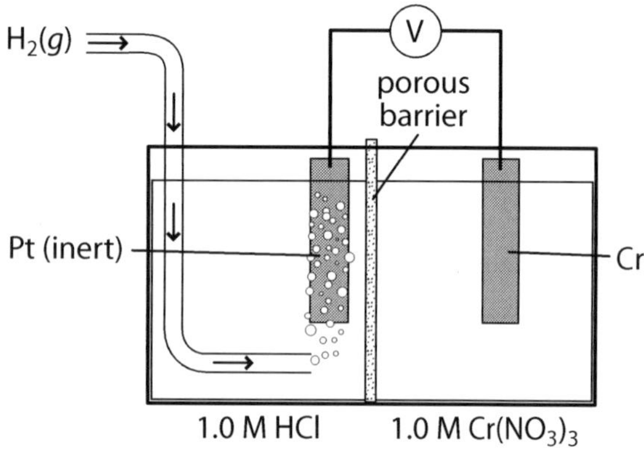

4. (a) Show the direction of electron flow on the above diagram.
   (b) In which half-cell does reduction occur?
   (c) Write the half-cell reactions involved.

5. (a) Label the anode and the cathode.

   (b) What is the expected initial voltage?

   (c) Describe the flow of ions within the cell.

   (d) Describe how the mass of each electrode changes as the cell operates.

6. (a) Draw a Zn | Zn^{2+} || F_2 | F^- electrochemical cell with the following labels:
   - electrodes (Zn, F_2)
   - solutions (1 M $ZnCl_2$, 1 M NaF)
   - anode and the cathode

   (b) Show the direction of electron flow on your diagram.
   (c) Show the direction of anion and cation flow on your diagram.
   (d) Write the cell's two half-reactions and overall redox reaction.

   (e) Calculate the cell's initial voltage.

7. What is the purpose of a salt bridge in an electrochemical cell?

8. Calculate the standard cell potential for the reaction: $Br_2 + 2\ Fe^{2+} \rightarrow 2\ Br^- + 2\ Fe^{3+}$

9. Suppose that the silver-silver ion electrode were used as the reference for E° values, instead of the hydrogen electrode. What would be the standard reduction potentials, E°, for these half-cell reactions?

(a) $F_2(g) + 2e^- \rightleftharpoons 2\ F^-$

(b) $Mg^{2+} + 2e^- \rightleftharpoons Mg(s)$

10. The standard cell potential for the following reaction is 2.33 V.

$$Sr + Cr^{2+} \rightarrow Sr^{2+} + Cr$$

Write the reduction half-reaction and determine its standard reduction potential (E°).

11. Given:

$Pd^{2+} + Cu \rightarrow Pd + Cu^{2+}$ E° = 0.49 V

$2\ Np + 3\ Pd^{2+} \rightarrow 2\ Np^{3+} + 3\ Pd$ E° = 2.73 V

(a) What is the standard reduction potential (E°) of Pd^{2+}?

(b) What is the standard reduction potential (E°) of Np^{3+}?

12. In the table below, fill in the missing cell voltages by using the voltages provided for other combinations of half-cells.

		Reduction Half-Cell	
		$Cd^{2+} + 2e^- \rightarrow Cd$	$Pt^{2+} + 2e^- \rightarrow Pt$
Oxidation Half-cell	$Pt \rightarrow Pt^{2+} + 2e^-$		0 V
	$Ni \rightarrow Ni^{2+} + 2e^-$	– 0.17 V	+ 1.43 V
	$Ce \rightarrow Ce^{3+} + 3e^-$	+ 1.93 V	

13. In an Fe(*s*) | Fe^{2+}(*aq*) || Pb^{2+}(*aq*) | Pb(*s*) standard cell, electrons are transferred from the Fe half-cell to the Pb half-cell.
   (a) What would be the effect on the voltage if $Pb(NO_3)_2$ were added to the lead half-cell?

   (b) What is the voltmeter reading when the cell reaches "equilibrium"?

   (c) What would be the effect on the voltage if sulfide ions (S^{2-}) were added to the Fe^{2+} ion compartment?

   (d) What would be the effect on the voltage if the size of the Fe electrode were doubled?

14. Sony demonstrated a paper cell at the Eco-Products 2011 Exhibition in Tokyo. Sony's bio-cell uses cellulase enzymes to hydrolyze paper into glucose, which is then oxidized. What features of this cell make it eco-friendly when compared to current commercial cells?

15. Describe how cathodic protection could be used to protect a steel stairway exposed to an ocean spray. Explain how this works.

16. Some steel nails are galvanized. Zinc is easier to oxidize than iron so how can coating a steel nail with zinc prevent it from corroding?

17. What adaptation to collision theory is necessary for redox reactions occurring in electrochemical cells?

18. Explain the graphic relationship shown here for the Danielli cell:

$Zn(s) + Cu^{2+}(aq) \rightarrow Zn^{2+}(aq) + Cu(s) \quad E^\circ_{cell} = 1.10\ V$

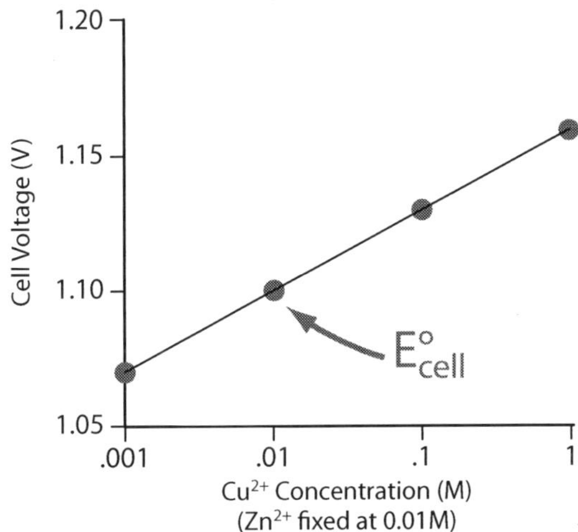

19. Use Table A7 Standard Reduction Potential of Half-Cells in the appendix to determine E° and *K* for the following reaction performed under standard conditions:

$I_2(s) + 5\ Cu^{2+}(aq) + 6\ H_2O(l) \rightarrow 2\ IO_3^-(aq) + 5\ Cu(s) + 12\ H^+(aq)$

20. (a) Calculate the voltage of the cell described by the following reaction. Then determine *K*. Assume standard temperature.

$2\ Al(s) + 3\ I_2(s) \rightarrow 2\ Al^{3+}(aq)\ (0.0040\ M) + 6\ I^-(aq)\ (0.010\ M)$

(b) How do these values compare to those for the cell operating under standard conditions? Explain.

21. Consider a cell in which the following reaction occurs at 25°C:

$Zn(s) + 2\ H^+(aq) \rightarrow Zn^{2+}(aq) + H_2(g)$

(a) Calculate E°_{cell}.

(b) If the $[Zn^{2+}]$ is 0.10 M and $[H_2]$ is 1.0 M and the measured cell voltage is 0.542 V, what is the hydrogen ion concentration?

(c) What is the pH?

22. Examine the electrochemical cell shown here.

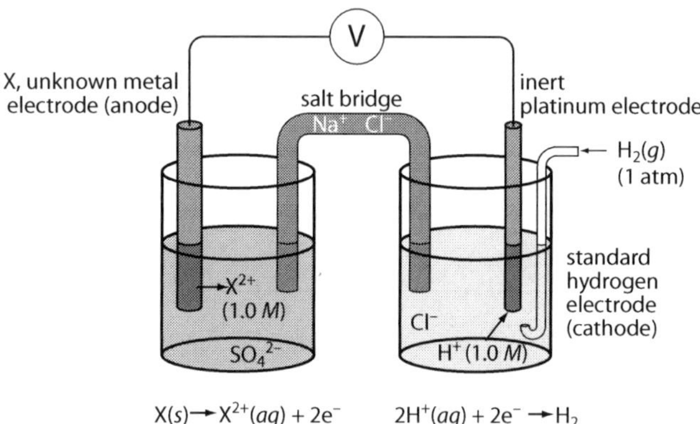

Under standard conditions, the equilibrium constant *K* for the cell's reaction is 6.1×10^8.

(a) What is E°_{cell}?

(b) What is the oxidation potential for the unknown metal?

(c) Identify the unknown metal.

7.4 Activity: Protecting the Environment for Future Generations

Question

How can you educate your family and school community about the potential environmental damage of burying dead batteries in your local landfill?

Background

You should never throw batteries in your household garbage. California residents have had a law prohibiting them from throwing batteries in their garbage since 2006. Batteries may contain toxic heavy metals such as mercury, cadmium, lithium, nickel, lead, and zinc, as well as corrosive electrolytes. When the casings of the batteries buried in our landfills corrode, these materials can leach into the groundwater. It is estimated that over 500 tonnes of dead batteries are being buried in North American landfills every day, yet recycling dead batteries would cost less than $4 per household per year.

Procedure

1. Set up a place in your house where your family members can dispose of their dead batteries (e.g., a plastic pail in the furnace room).
2. Find out the location of a disposal/recycling facility in your community where batteries are accepted.
3. Organize a one-week battery collection blitz in your school. Use your school announcements about the event to teach the staff and students at your school not to throw batteries into the garbage.

Results and Discussion

1. Household location for battery disposal: ______________________________

2. Community location for battery disposal: ______________________________

3. Number of batteries collected in school blitz: ____________

4. Mass of batteries collected in school blitz: ________ kg

5. Was this activity a success? ______

   Why or why not? ______________________________

   ____

   ____

7.5 The Electrolytic Cell

1. Specialty sports drinks are called electrolyte drinks because they replenish the water and solutes, including electrolytes, that athletes lose in sweat during exercise. Which of the following ingredients of a typical sports drink are electrolytes: water, sucrose, dextrose, citric acid, sodium chloride, sodium citrate, and potassium dihydrogen phosphate?

2. Draw a type 1 electrolytic cell electrolyzing molten NaCl. Label the DC source, its terminals, and the anode and cathode of the electrolytic cell. Show each ion in the molten NaCl migrating toward the appropriate electrode. Write the half-reaction that occurs at each electrode and predict the voltage required to operate this cell.

3. Sodium is commercially produced by the electrolysis of molten NaCl in an apparatus called a Downs cell. A Downs cell directs the products into separate chambers to prevent them from coming into contact with each other. Why is it important to keep the two products physically separated as the cell operates?

4. Complete the following table:

	Cell Type (1,2,3)	Electrolyte	Anode/Cathode	Products	
				Anode	Cathode
(a)		$NaCl(l)$	Pt/Pt		
(b)		$NaCl(aq)$	Pt/C		
(c)		$CuBr_2(aq)$	C/C		
(d)		$AlF_3(aq)$	C/C		
(e)		$CuCl_2(aq)$	Cu/Cu		

5. An electrolytic cell contains inert electrodes in a solution of acidified copper(II) nitrate.
   (a) Write the half-reactions occurring at the anode and cathode.

   (b) Predict the voltage required to operate this cell.

6. Electrolysis is also used as a technique for the permanent removal of individual hairs. A very thin metal probe is inserted alongside the hair into the follicle beneath the skin's surface from which the hair emerges. This probe is the cathode of an electrolytic cell. Hydroxide ions formed at the cathode kill the cells that produce the hair. Write the half-reaction that produces the hydroxide ions.

7. How is electrorefining a special kind of electrowinning?

8. Why is it uneconomical to produce metallic aluminum by electrolyzing $Al_2O_3(l)$ and impossible to produce metallic aluminum by electrolyzing $Al_2O_3(aq)$?

9. Describe how impressed current cathodic protection is electrochemically different than galvanic cathodic protection.

10. Draw a type 3 electrolytic cell electroplating an aluminum spoon with silver. Label the DC source, its terminals, and the anode and cathode of the electrolytic cell. Predict the voltage required to operate this cell.

11. An electrolytic cell containing inert electrodes is used to electrolyze pure water.
   (a) What type of cell is this? Explain.

   (b) Identify a salt that could be added to water to increase its conductivity without the salt reacting.

12. What is the minimum voltage theoretically required to operate an electrolytic cell consisting of inert electrodes in an aqueous solution of $CuBr_2$?

7.5 Activity: Location, Location, Location

Question

What criteria would a multinational corporation use when deciding where to locate an aluminum smelter?

Background

In 2015, North America produced 4.44 million tonnes of aluminum worth about $6.6 billion. This makes us the world's third largest primary producer of aluminum, just behind the Gulf States 5.1 million tonnes and far behind China's 31.6 million tonnes.

Procedure

1. Reread the section on the Héroult-Hall process for producing aluminum.
2. There is a saying that the three most important criteria when purchasing real estate are location, location, and location. But what factors make one location more desirable than another? Imagine that you are the CEO of a multinational corporation planning to build an aluminum smelter. In the table provided below, list five important criteria that you would use when deciding where to build your smelter.

Results and Discussion

1.

Five Criteria for Choosing a Site

2. Look at the criteria of some of your classmates. Identify an important criterion that you didn't include in your table.

3. Kitimat, a coastal city in the Pacific Northwest, is a company town that was designed and built by the Aluminum Company of Canada (Alcan) in the 1950s. The Rio Tinto Alcan smelter is undergoing a $6 billion modernization and expansion that was completed in 2014. The conversion of Kitimat's smelter will make it the "greenest" aluminum smelter in the world. Use the five criteria you listed in the above table to rate Kitimat as a location for an aluminum smelter.

7.6 The Stoichiometry of Electrochemistry – Faraday's Constant and Free Energy

1. Electroplating metals makes them more resistant to corrosion and may make them more attractive.
   (a) A motorcycle's exhaust pipe is plated with chromium by passing 55 A of current through a cell containing chromium(III) ions for 0.75 min. What mass of chromium is deposited on the pipe?

   (b) Steel screws for use in kitchen cabinetry are plated with nickel from a nickel(II) ion solution. If 125 mg of nickel are required for each screw and a current of 0.50 A is used, how long will it take to plate 32 screws for a set of kitchen cabinets?

   (c) An antique teapot requires a new silver surface with a mass of 12.0 g. If the plating process requires 1.50 h, what current should be used?

2. "Tin" cans are prepared by plating a steel can with tin.
   (a) What is the advantage of placing a layer of tin against the steel, which is mainly composed of iron?

   (b) The steel can is connected at the cathode in an electrolytic cell containing 1.00 L of 3.75 mol/L $SnCl_2(aq)$. A current of 2.50 A passes through the cell for 1.25 h.
   (i) What mass of tin is deposited on the steel can?

   (ii) What concentration of $SnCl_2(aq)$ remains in the cell once the plating is complete?

3. Pure bismuth is produced by the electrolysis of a solution containing BiO^+ ions. How long would it take to produce 15.0 g of bismuth using 10.0 A of current? Begin by writing a balanced reduction half reaction.

4. An aqueous solution of CoF_2 is electrolyzed with 3.50 A for 1.40 h. Both electrodes are made of graphite.
   (a) What mass of cobalt metal is collected?

   (b) What volume of oxygen gas evolves at the other electrode? Determine the volume at STP conditions.

   (c) Give two chemical tests to determine that the gas is, indeed, oxygen.

5. Calculate the standard cell potential E° *and* the change in free energy $\Delta G°$ for each of these reactions. Which reaction is spontaneous?
   (a) $2\ H_2O(l) \rightarrow 2\ H_2(g) + O_2(g)$ *decomposition of water*

   (b) $2\ Fe(s) + O_2(g) + 4\ H^+(aq) \rightarrow 2\ Fe^{2+}(aq) + 2\ H_2O(l)$ *rusting of Fe*

6. The reaction $Ag_2O(s) + Zn(s) + H_2O(l) \rightarrow 2\ Ag(s) + Zn^{2+}(aq) + 2\ OH^-(aq)$ occurs in some "button" batteries producing a cell potential of 1.104 V.
   (a) Calculate the standard reduction potential for the cathodic half reaction.

   (b) Calculate $\Delta G°$ for the spontaneous redox reaction.

7. The reaction $CH_4(g) + 2\,O_2(g) + 2\,OH^-(aq) \rightarrow CO_3^{2-}(aq) + 3\,H_2O(l)$ occurs in a methane-oxygen fuel cell producing energy at nearly 70% efficiency (compared to the 25% efficiency of a normal combustion reaction to produce steam in an electricity generating plant). E°_{cell} is 0.23 V for this reaction.

   (a) Calculate ΔG° for this reaction.

   (b) Given $E^\circ = 0.40$ V for $O_2(g) + 2\,H_2O(l) + 4\,e^- \rightarrow 4\,OH^-(aq)$, write the balanced oxidation half-reaction and determine E° for the anodic reaction.

8. If 0.40 g of a metal is deposited on a cathode by 5.0 A of current in 0.50 h, what mass of the *same* metal would be deposited by 1 faraday? Recall: 1 faraday is equivalent to 1 mole of electrons *or* 96 500 C.

9. Scientists and engineers have designed a wide variety of new rechargeable cells during the decade 2004 to 2014. A popular, though expensive, example is the silver-cadmium cell. The overall reaction is:
   $2\,AgO(s) + H_2O(l) + Cd(s) \rightarrow Ag_2O(s) + Cd(OH)_2(s)\ \Delta G^\circ = -257\ kJ/mol_{rxn}$
   What is the voltage for a silver-cadmium cell?

10. Scientists designed the first "transistor battery" shown here in the 1950s. It was commonly used to power the first portable transistor radios. Today, devices such as remote control cars, alarm systems, motion sensors, and smoke detectors use this same battery. The battery is actually a system of *six cells* each involving the standard dry cell reaction shown here:

$$2\,MnO_2(s) + H_2O(l) + Zn(s) \rightarrow Mn_2O_3(s) + 2\,OH^-(aq) + Zn^{2+}(aq)$$

$\Delta G°$ for this reaction is –299 kJ/mol$_{rxn}$. What is the overall voltage for a transistor battery?

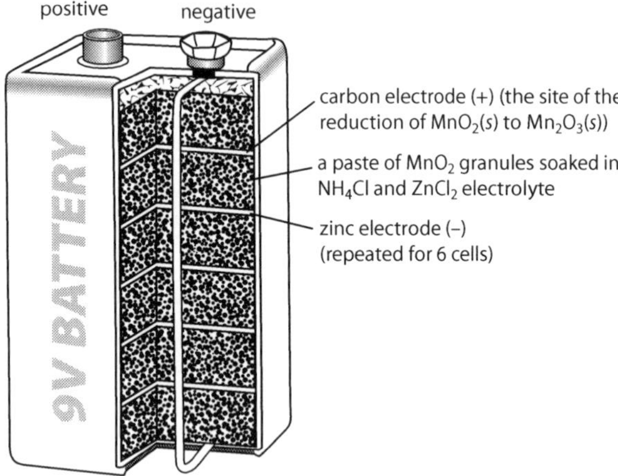

A transistor battery consists of six cells stacked vertically and connected in series.

11. The Hall-Héroult cell requires a low-voltage DC source (approximately 4.53 V) that applies current across inert graphite electrodes through molten bauxite (Al_2O_3) ore. The addition of cryolite (Na_3AlF_6) lowers the melting point of bauxite.

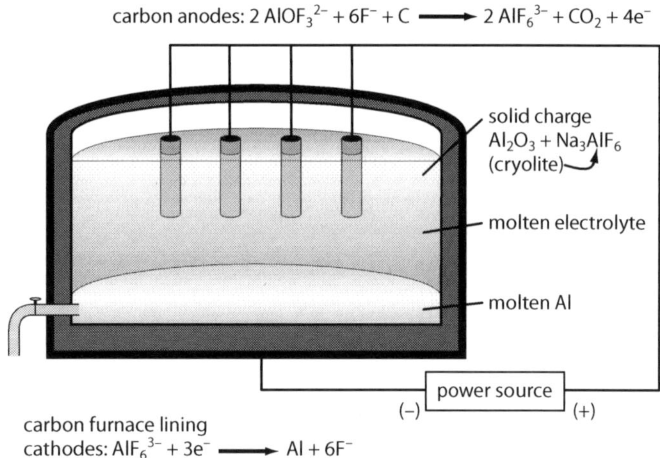

The Hall-Héroult process for the production of aluminum metal.

(a) Combine the anode and cathode half-reactions to give the overall equation for the Hall-Héroult process.

(b) Calculate the $\Delta G°$ value for the process.

Appendix — Reference Tables

Table A1 Atomic Masses of the Elements

Table A2 Names, Formulas, and Charges of Some Common Ions

Table A3 Solubility of Common Compounds in Water

Table A4 Solubility Product Constants at 25°C

Table A5 Relative Strengths of Brønsted-Lowry Acids and Bases

Table A6 Acid-Base Indicators

Table A7 Standard Reduction Potentials of Half-Cells

Table A8 Thermodynamic Data at 25°C for Assorted Substances

Scan this QR code to access
Tables A1 through A8

Answer Key

For the most current version of the answer key, scan the appropriate QR code with your mobile device. Or, go to edvantagescience.com, login and select AP Chemistry 2 Workbook*PLUS*. The answer keys are posted in each chapter.

Chapter 1

Chapter 2

Chapter 3

Chapter 4

Chapter 5

Chapter 6

Chapter 7

Made in the USA
Columbia, SC
20 July 2018